Umbrella Guide to

Oregon Lighthouses

by
Sharlene & Ted Nelson

UMBRELLA
BOOKS ®

An imprint of Epicenter Press

Editor: Christine Ummel
Cover design: Elizabeth Watson
Cover photo: Umpqua River Lighthouse at dusk, by Wood Sabold
Pre-press production: Newman Design/Illustration
Printer: McNaughton & Gunn

To order single copies of
UMBRELLA GUIDE TO OREGON LIGHTHOUSES,
send $10.95 (Washington residents add $.90 sales tax) plus $2 for
book rate shipping to: Epicenter Press, Box 82368, Kenmore Station,
Seattle, WA 98028. Ask for our catalog. BOOKSELLERS: Retail
discounts are available from our trade distributor, Graphic Arts
Center Publishing Co., Portland, OR. Call 800-452-3032.

PRINTED IN THE UNITED STATES OF AMERICA
First printing, June 1994
10 9 8 7 6 5 4

Foreword

With this delightful book, *Umbrella Guide to Oregon Lighthouses*, Sharlene and Ted Nelson have added a worthy companion to their previous guides to the lighthouses of California and Washington.

This guide tells the story of the lighthouses which served the Oregon Coast and the lower Columbia River, the Columbia River Lightship Station, and the lighthouse tenders that supplied them, all woven nicely into the rich maritime history of the Beaver State. The informative chapters on the Fresnel lens and the fog signals, written in a clear and concise manner, will enhance a visit to any lighthouse.

As with their other lighthouse guides, they have included maps as well as access information for those stations open to the public.

The book includes current and historic photos, and provides facts not published before. It is a must for any lighthouse enthusiast's library and for visitors to the Oregon Coast.

Wayne C. Wheeler, President
U.S. Lighthouse Society

Acknowledgments

Without the help of many, we could not have written this book. They were giving of their time and knowledge, and we want to thank them all.

At the United States Lighthouse Society in San Francisco, Wayne Wheeler was generous with his expertise, and he and Bill Morrison opened the society's library and files to us.

Coast Guard Museum Northwest curator Gene Davis and volunteers Larry Dubia and D. A. Webb provided hard-to-find facts and rare photos.

Members of the United States Coast Guard 13th District, Stan Norman (retired), Dan J. Long, Kenneth E. McLain, and Kevin J. Owens, provided tours and current information.

Archivists in Washington, D.C., William Sherman, Angie Spicer VanDereedt, and James G. Cassidy searched out original documents.

More information came from directors of historical societies, museum curators, and historians: Helen Barton, Bill Brainard, M. Wayne Jensen, Jr., Billie Ivey, Ann Koppy, Paul Kuper, Dorothy Mills, John Quay, Fred J. Reenstjerna, Susan Seyl, Sieglinde Smith, Mikki Tint, Dorothy Wall, Kris White, and Anne Witty.

The future status of the lighthouses was given by state and federal personnel: Elizabeth Potter, Jane Cottrel-Henifen, Steven J. Gobat, and Michael Hewitt.

Family members of lighthouse keepers and builders who assisted us were Helga Settles, Irene and Bob DeRoy, and Tom Hillstrom. And, thanks to optical expert Larry Hardin, Tony Hostetter, and Theresea Hewitt.

Table of Contents

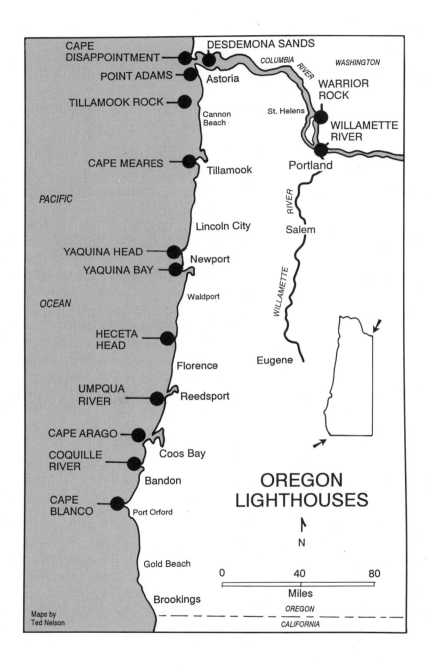

CAPE
DISAPPOINTMENT

DESDEMONA SANDS

COLUMBIA RIVER

WASHINGTON

POINT ADAMS

Astoria

WARRIOR
ROCK

TILLAMOOK ROCK

Cannon
Beach

St. Helens

WILLAMETTE
RIVER

CAPE MEARES

Tillamook

Portland

PACIFIC

Lincoln City

RIVER

Salem

YAQUINA HEAD

YAQUINA BAY

Newport

OCEAN

Waldport

WILLAMETTE

HECETA
HEAD

Florence

Eugene

UMPQUA
RIVER

Reedsport

CAPE ARAGO

Coos Bay

COQUILLE
RIVER

Bandon

OREGON
LIGHTHOUSES

CAPE
BLANCO

Port Orford

N

Gold Beach

0   40   80

Miles

Brookings

OREGON

CALIFORNIA

Maps by
Ted Nelson

vi

Introduction

Travelers along the Oregon Coast and to a headland north of the Columbia River are treated to a spectacular view of lighthouse history. From Cape Blanco in the south to Cape Disappointment in the north, there are nine lighthouses, the oldest dating back to 1856. Each one is within a few miles of U.S. Highway 101.

These nine lighthouses, and one that can be seen on an offshore rock, are the survivors of fourteen lighthouse stations built to guide mariners along the Oregon Coast and up the Columbia River to Portland. They had their beginning when the Pacific Northwest became a U.S. Territory in 1848.

When the territory was established, the Oregon Coast was the domain of Native Americans. They fished the coastal rivers, canoed its bays, and dug for shellfish on long, sandy beaches.

But along the lower Columbia and Willamette rivers, Oregon Trail immigrants had been building settlements, farms, and mills. With the 1848 discovery of gold in California, the lower rivers were becoming busy waterways. Ships crossed the treacherous Columbia River bar and sailed upriver to load lumber, flour, and produce for markets in San Francisco.

The settlers were so dependent on maritime trade that with the territorial act, Congress voted to construct a lighthouse on Cape Disappointment, at the Columbia River's entrance, and one at New Dungeness on the Strait of Juan de Fuca. It was the first official action to establish lighthouses on the West Coast.

Besides agreeing to build the new territory's lights, Congress stipulated that other potential lighthouse sites along the West Coast be investigated before construction began. The U.S. Coast Survey was selected to make the study.

The Coast Survey party arrived at San Francisco in the spring of 1849. They found its shores lined with abandoned vessels, their crews gone to the gold fields. The discovery of gold had caused maritime traffic along California's coast to burgeon.

The Coast Survey investigated potential lighthouse locations from the Strait of Juan de Fuca to San Diego Bay. By 1851 they had recommended sixteen lighthouse sites: ten in California, five in what would become Washington state, including Cape Disappointment, and one at the mouth of Oregon's Umpqua River.

Construction of the first lighthouses began in 1853, but the completion of Cape Disappointment's lighthouse was delayed until 1856. The Umpqua River's lighthouse wasn't completed until 1857.

By then Oregon's coast was no longer the home of just Native Americans. Gold had been discovered in southwest Oregon. Ships carrying settlers and miners had crossed the bars of the Umpqua, Coos, and other coastal rivers.

Oregon's real "gold," however, lay in its vast resources of timber, salmon, agricultural products, and coal. Entrepreneurs had been quick to take advantage of California's early gold rush demand for these products. As maritime trade serving California and world markets expanded, more and more vessels were put at risk in Oregon's fogs and gales, and on dangerous river shoals and bars. These risks were gradually reduced as more lighthouses were built, and a lightship was anchored near the Columbia River's entrance.

The heart of the early lighthouses was the Fresnel (pronouced *Fraynell*) lens. Handcrafted in Europe, the lens' prisms focused light into a powerful beam. Until electricity came to the stations, the light for the lenses came from lamps burning a variety of fuels from whale oil to kerosene. In dense fogs, however, even the most powerful beam of light was useless, so some stations also had fog signals. (For more information on the Fresnel lens and fog signals, see Chapters 17 and 18.)

The soul of the lighthouse stations was their keepers. They tended the lights from dusk to dawn, often with the help of their families, and operated the fog signals. The keepers of the lightship lights were the crews who manned the stout little vessels.

Lighthouses and lightships were first built by the U.S. Lighthouse Board with funds authorized by Congress. The Board ran the U.S. Lighthouse Service, which was responsible for operating the lighthouses, the lightships, and the depots and tenders that serviced them.

In 1910 the Lighthouse Board was abolished, and a Bureau of Lighthouses was put in charge of the Lighthouse Service. In 1939 the lighthouse system became the responsibility of the U.S. Coast Guard. The Coast Guard began to increase the automation of the lights and fog signals in the 1960s. Some early Fresnel lenses were replaced with aero beacons or small plastic optics. No longer needed, the resident keepers gradually left their stations. A large buoy replaced the Columbia River Lightship. Many of the surviving lighthouses are in state parks or on other lands where they can be visited by the public. Some of the lighthouses have been restored by the State of Oregon, while others have been refurbished by the Coast Guard. Improved public access is planned for many of the stations. The last lightship to be stationed at the Columbia's entrance is moored at Astoria's Columbia River Maritime Museum.

This guide tells the story of Oregon's lighthouses, some still assisting mariners. It also tells the stories of the lightships, lighthouse tenders, keepers, and crews that together served Oregon's mariners for over one hundred years.

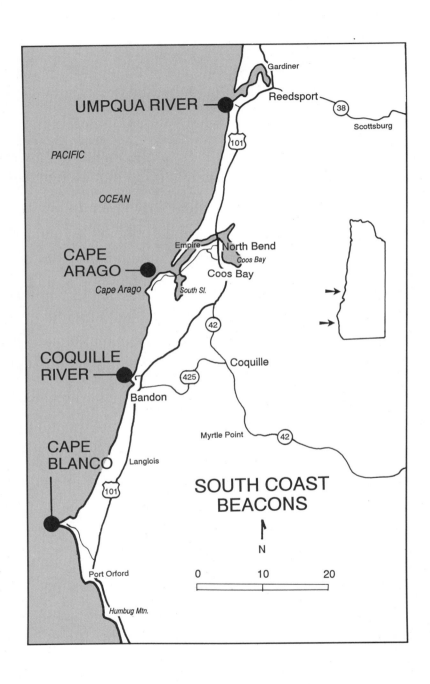

UMPQUA RIVER •————— Gardiner

Reedsport

38

Scottsburg

PACIFIC

101

OCEAN

Empire — North Bend

Coos Bay

CAPE
ARAGO •—————

Coos Bay

Cape Arago

South Sl.

42

COQUILLE
RIVER •—————

Coquille

425

Bandon

Myrtle Point

42

CAPE
BLANCO

Langlois

101

SOUTH COAST
BEACONS

↑
N

Port Orford

0   10   20

Humbug Mtn.

Section 1

South Coast Beacons

The south coast of Oregon was the first Pacific Northwest shore to be reached by Europeans. When not battered by storms or caught in "thicke and stinking fogges," as Francis Drake called them, explorers could see mountains shouldering to the surf, terraced capes, and a great sweep of dunes with the Coast Range rising behind.

Spanish explorer Bartolome Ferrelo may have come this far north from Mexico in 1543. Drake came in 1579 after plundering Spanish galleons on their way from Manila to Mexico. By then, the myth of a Northwest Passage connecting the Atlantic with the Pacific had gained widespread acceptance. Drake was followed by the Spanish explorers Sebastian Viscaino and Martin d'Aguilar who sought the passage in 1603.

It wasn't until the eighteenth century that explorers again sailed this coast. Then more Spanish, English, and French mariners passed this way, seeking new territories and searching for the fabled passage. They were followed by English and American fur traders.

In the 1850s settlers were enticed to the south coast by the accessibility that the Umpqua River offered to interior mines and valleys, and by the gold that had been discovered in coastal beach sands. As small settlements grew, they became dependent on shipbuilding and exporting lumber, coal, fish, and farm produce.

The first lighthouse to be built in what would become Oregon was established on the Umpqua River in 1857. Later, lighthouses were built at Cape Blanco, at the mouth of the Coquille River, and at Cape Arago. Each station, in its unique fashion, survives today.

TED NELSON

The Cape Blanco seacoast tower, built in 1870, is Oregon's oldest.

Chapter 1

Cape Blanco Lighthouse

On December 20, 1870, Lighthouse Service engineer R. S. Williamson, sitting in his San Francisco office, received good news about the Cape Blanco Lighthouse. Excited about what he had heard, he wrote a letter to Admiral W. B. Shubrick, Chairman of the Lighthouse Board.

"I have the honor to report that the L.H. Tender Shubrick has returned from Cape Blanco and has brought down the machinist and the remainder of the employees," wrote Williamson. "I have no reason to doubt that it [the light] will be exhibited for the first time tonight." He was right. That night the keepers touched a lucerne to the new lamp, and a fixed white light beamed from the first-order Fresnel lens in the fifty-nine-foot tower. Today Cape Blanco's light still shines from the oldest original tower on the Oregon Coast.

A lighthouse was badly needed on Cape Blanco, a broad spur projecting about one and a half miles from the coastline north of Port Orford. The cape received some of the coast's worst weather: thick fogs in the summer, gale winds and heavy rains in winter. In 1869 Williamson reported that the cape's rainfall was "equalled at only two other points in the United States where records are kept." Also, in the waters beyond the cape's 200-foot cliffs lay jagged rocks and ledges. Some were hidden just below the sea's surface, creating dangerous sailing conditions.

When a lighthouse on the cape was proposed in 1864, there were no lighthouses in the state. The first Umpqua River Lighthouse had succumbed to erosion, and the tower at Cape Arago was yet to be built. Except

3

for ordering a first-order Fresnel lens from the French firm of Barbier and Fenstre, little was done to build the lighthouse until 1868.

That year Williamson contracted for bricks to be made from a local clay deposit. He also received plans from the Lighthouse Board for a short tower and a large dwelling. He rejected both. A site survey revealed a higher tower was needed so the light could be seen by vessels approaching from the south. Also, Williamson decided the proposed dwelling was too large and expensive. He requested and received new plans for a taller tower and a smaller dwelling.

The first building materials arrived in May 1870 on board the schooner *Bunkalation.* Part of its cargo had been landed safely on the south beach below the cape when gale winds struck. The storm drove the ship onto the beach; it and the remaining cargo were a total loss.

A new shipment arrived in July. Once the material was landed, it was hauled up the steep bluff. By December 15 the tall, cone-shaped tower and the dwelling, which had a fireplace in nearly every room, were completed. The first principal keeper, H. B. Burnap, and his two assistants, J. Bond and Nathan Cook, moved in.

Burnap had been the last keeper at the Umpqua River Lighthouse. He and his family then moved to Port Orford, where they were living when Burnap was assigned to Cape Blanco. Assistant Nathan Cook came from California. To reach his new assignment, Cook rode horseback from Crescent City. He became lost in the coastal wilderness before arriving at Cape Blanco.

During the station's first years, delivering supplies to the keepers was hazardous. The beach on the south side of the cape was exposed to southerly winds. Often they began to blow while cargo was being unloaded, and the tender had to leave quickly. The beach road to Port Orford crossed quicksand and was only passable at low tide. In 1886 a new road was built that led east through the forest. When it was completed, supplies were landed at Port Orford and hauled by wagon to the station.

With its isolation, fogs, and winds, Cape Blanco was not a favorite station for many keepers. James Langlois and James Hughes were exceptions. Both were sons of local pioneers, and their overlapping careers at the cape spanned nearly a half century.

Langlois became first assistant under Charles Peirce in 1875. Peirce, his wife Sarah, and their six children had arrived earlier from Yaquina

Bay's lighthouse. When the Peirces left in 1883, Langlois was promoted to principal keeper.

Langlois, like other keepers, received visits from the Lighthouse Inspector. In the summer of 1888 the inspector stayed two days. He gave Langlois good marks: "the lamps, lens, and tower were clean and neat and in good order...." The inspector also noted, however, that one of the assistant keepers was wearing the wrong hat with his Lighthouse Service uniform.

That same year twenty-five-year-old James Hughes became the first assistant. In 1889 he married Laura McMullan, and brought his bride to Cape Blanco. By the late 1890s the Langlois family had five children and the Hughes had two. These two families, living together with the second assistant keeper, were outgrowing the dwelling. The inspector recommended that a second one be built. He repeated his request to the Lighthouse Board every year for over eight years, until a new dwelling finally was added.

In the meantime, Hughes solved his housing problem by buying a 500-acre dairy ranch on the Sixes River. He, Laura, and their two daughters moved into the ranch's large, ten-room house. It was not far from his father's Victorian home, which still stands near the road to the lighthouse.

With the help of Laura and two hired ranch hands, Hughes worked as a rancher as well as a lighthouse keeper. He once told a reporter, "There isn't much money in my lighthouse job, but it doesn't take up much of my time and I like it." He walked or rode horseback to the lighthouse to stand his watch, and spent his mornings performing his keeper's duties. In the afternoon he tended his ranch and his purebred Jersey cows.

One of the first women to tend an Oregon lighthouse, Mrs. Mabel Bretherton, joined Langlois and Hughes as a second assistant keeper in 1903. The wife of a keeper at the Coquille River Lighthouse, Bretherton had been on duty at Cape Blanco for only a few months when a ship was lost nearby.

On an October afternoon, the steamship *South Portland* was on its way to San Francisco carrying fourteen passengers, twenty-five crewmen, and a cargo of grain. In the dense fog, the ship hit a sunken reef and immediately began to fill with water. The captain, J. B. McIntrye, jumped into the first boat to leave the sinking ship.

The next day Langlois recorded in the station log: "21 persons lost with the wreck, ship sinking in about three quarters of an hour after striking. Ship a total loss . . . Keeper patrolled the beach north and south of the station but found nothing of the wreck or any of the drowned crew or passengers."

For several days the keepers continued to walk the beaches. Oscar Langlois, the keeper's son, found an oar and a stool from the ship. Bretherton found an officer's coat with anchors on the collar a mile north of the station. Captain McIntrye later was ruled criminally negligent for abandoning his ship before seeing to the safety of his passengers.

Bretherton continued as an assistant keeper until she was transferred in 1905 to Washington's North Head Lighthouse. Langlois, after forty-two years with the Lighthouse Service, retired in 1918 and moved to Bandon. He knew he didn't need to worry about the care and upkeep of the Cape Blanco Lighthouse. After thirty years as the first assistant keeper, Hughes was promoted to principal keeper. He was dedicated to the lighthouse and apparently couldn't bear to stay away from it for long. A December 24, 1920, log entry records that "J. S. Hughes departed 6 A.M. - 8 days shore liberty - Returned 2 days later." Hughes retired to his ranch a few years afterward.

Lighthouses have always attracted visitors, and Cape Blanco was no exception. Between 1896 and 1916, while Langlois and Hughes were keepers, more than 4,000 people signed the guest book. Visitors were welcome except in times of war. During World War II, the Coast Guard issued orders that Cape Blanco "will be a defense area with coastal lookout and the public will be restricted. . . . "

Then the lighthouse attracted a visitor of a different kind. Albert Anderson, a civilian keeper at Cape Blanco during the war, recalled the summer of 1942 in a later interview. A Japanese submarine, standing off the coast, launched a small float plane. The pilot used the lighthouse to navigate by, flying inland twice to drop incendiary bombs in the forest.

Other unwelcome visitors came after the light was automated. In November 1992 vandals broke into the lighthouse. With a sledgehammer, they broke six of the lens' prism pieces and knocked out one of its eight bullseyes (circular, convex lenses). The Coast Guard turned on an emergency light until the lens, minus a bullseye, was operating again. Later, two local teenage boys were apprehended and convicted for the vandalism.

The Coast Guard then searched the nation for an optical company to repair the lens — and found Hardin Optical in Bandon, just twenty-six miles away. Owner Larry Hardin looked at the lens and agreed to try to repair it.

Hardin first searched for glass similar to the original in appearance and optical characteristics. Corning Pyrex™ provided the closest match, but didn't work perfectly. "When we ground the bullseye to the original dimensions, it produced a different focal length," explained Hardin. The lens was ground again with a slightly different curvature. In the meantime, the firm had to invent new machinery to duplicate the prisms. By the spring of 1994 the lens was whole again. The local firm had successfully recreated parts of a lens designed 172 years before.

This repaired Fresnel lens is the lighthouse's second. The original first-order lens produced a constant beam of light. About 1909 a hood was placed around the lamp. It was raised and lowered by a clockwork mechanism to produce a flashing light.

In 1936 the original lens was replaced with the present rotating lens. Slightly smaller than the first lens, it produces a flashing light at twenty-second intervals. The last known record

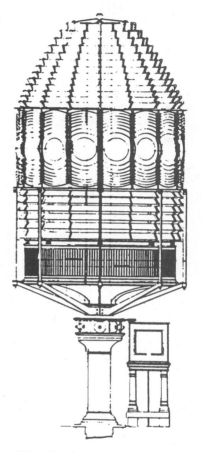

The circular lenses in the panels of a rotating Fresnel lens, called "bullseyes," have been the target of vandals at two of Oregon's lighthouses.

of the original lens is a set of instructions written to principal keeper O. E. Hayward, arranging for its shipment to the Tongue Point Lighthouse Depot.

Today the lighthouse tower and its workroom, built with 200,000 bricks, are all that remain of the original station. A vacated Coast Guard duplex and electronics building stand nearby. Though the station is closed, it can be seen from a viewpoint at the end of the park road.

Directions and Hours: The lighthouse is about five miles west of Highway 101. Watch for "Cape Blanco State Park" signs near Milepost 297. The park is open daily, and there are plans to eventually open the lighthouse for tours. For more information, phone (503) 332-6744 or write to the Friends of Cape Blanco, P.O. Box 285, Sixes, OR 97476.

Chapter 2

Coquille River Lighthouse

The Coquille River Lighthouse, its original light and fog signal gone, stands above the rocks and sand of the river's north jetty across from Bandon. It was the last lighthouse built on the Oregon Coast and served as a harbor and coast light. Though abandoned by the Coast Guard in 1939, it can be visited today.

The lighthouse's architectural style, with elements of High Victorian Italiante, is unique among West Coast lighthouses. It is a small, angular building with an attached tower, a low pyramidal roof, and arched window heads. The main floor housed a fog signal.

In the mid-1800s, many vessels by-passed the Coquille River, even though early settlers in the Coquille River Valley, about thirty miles upstream, had produce to ship. Rocks and shifting sands at the river's entrance — sometimes with only three feet of water over the bar — kept vessels away.

Still, some captains took the risks. In the summer of 1859, the schooner *Twin Sisters,* with Captain Rackleff at the helm, braved the bar and sailed about forty miles up the river. In the 1860s other captains crossed the bar to load lumber from upriver sawmills for shipment to San Francisco. Nonetheless, local citizens wanted more maritime commerce on the river and recognized they needed an inducement for shippers—an improved river bar.

After several years of lobbying, they were jubilant when Congress passed a bill in 1880 to improve the mouth of the Coquille River. A jetty built on the south side of the bar created a channel ten feet deep. The

TED NELSON

A visitor looks seaward from the fog signal room of the Coquille River Lighthouse.

improvements did bring more vessels; "in the seasons of 1883, 1884, 1885, one hundred and sixty-six coasting vessels entered the river," reported the 1889 *Coast Pilot*.

To guide the increasing traffic, Congressman B. Hermann, an avid supporter of improved navigation on Oregon's coast, introduced a bill in 1886 to establish a lighthouse at the river's mouth. Several years passed while committee hearings took place and engineers filed studies regarding the need for a Coquille River light. Congress authorized construction of the lighthouse in 1891, but more delays followed. The landowners at first were reluctant to sell, and the station's plans were not ready.

Men, tools, and materials finally arrived at the site in the spring of 1895. Some of the men leveled the top of Rackleff Rock where the lighthouse would stand, while others cut local stone for the structure's foundation. When the station was completed, a long wooden walkway stretched across the sand, connecting the lighthouse with a spacious, wood-frame duplex dwelling. Nearby stood a barn encircled by a wire fence for keeping cows and chickens.

Two keepers, transferred from the Heceta Head Lighthouse, arrived with their families. J. Frank Barker was assigned principal keeper, and John M. Cowan was his assistant. On February 29, 1896, they lit the lamp in the fourth-order Fresnel lens for the first time. The fixed white light, shining for twenty-eight seconds with an eclipse of two seconds, could be seen for nearly thirteen miles.

The next day, while Barker and Cowan cleaned the lens, snow began to fall. Blown by strong northwest winds, the snow thickened, reducing visibility. Barker and Cowan decided to fire up the new fog signal. They did, and March 1 became the official date for the fog signal's start-up.

Barker, like other keepers, was required to keep a daily log book. Most entries described the weather, daily duties, or the transfer of keepers. Occasionally a tragedy was recorded, written in the same matter-of-fact style as other entries. On April 1, 1896, Barker wrote, "Captain R. S. Littlefield, engineer in charge of jetties dropped dead while returning to his office after visiting this station."

In the log, keepers also noted the passage of ships across the river's bar and shipwrecks near the lighthouse. On January 9, 1897, the keeper wrote: "Schooner *Moro* stuck on the bar, had to throw overboard her

BANDON HISTORICAL SOCIETY

A long wooden walkway connected the keeper's dwelling with the lighthouse.

deckload of lumber, broom handles and fish." Even relieved of its cargo, the ship could not be freed and was a total loss.

The three-masted schooner *Advance* was luckier. In late 1905 it rammed the north jetty, then under construction. Had it been a little closer, the ship's bowsprit would have struck the lighthouse. Ten days later the log notes: "Schooner *Advance* which went ashore in front of the lighthouse was taken off last night with very little injury."

During the lighthouse's first four years, turnover of the principal keepers occurred annually. Assistant Cowan, however, served until 1900. He, his wife, Mary, and their eight children left that spring for his new assignment as principal keeper at Cape Flattery. This isolated lighthouse on Washington's northern tip would be the Cowans' home for the next thirty-two years.

Unlike the keepers at Cape Flattery and many other West Coast lighthouses, the keepers at the Coquille River station did not have a problem

12

with isolation. The small town of Bandon stood on the river's opposite shore. At night keepers could see its friendly lights glowing along the river and on the hillside above. Every day they took the station boat into town for supplies. One of the keeper's wives used the boat to take the children to school in Bandon. The boat couldn't get to town fast enough to beat the stork, however. Two girls were born at the lighthouse, one in 1916 and one in 1932.

Although the keepers were close to the comforts of town, the sand spit where they lived was bleak. Driftwood lay stacked on the nearby beach, and wind-blown sand swirled around the buildings. In 1901 the lighthouse superintendent filed a report: "Immense quantities of sand are frequently piled up around them [the dwelling and barn] rendering access to the different buildings difficult, and at times almost impossible."

He recommended that planking be built around the dwelling, as well as portable sand fences that could be moved as needed. Both projects were completed the following year. Still, this didn't keep family members from tracking sand into the parlors and kitchens. The keepers' wives, ever mindful of a surprise visit by the lighthouse inspector, laid flour sacks on the floors to keep them clean.

By 1915 more vessels were using the channel near the south jetty, and the Bureau of Lighthouses proposed moving the light and fog signal to the river's south side. Shippers, however, were accustomed to the lighthouse's location. They protested, and the lighthouse got a reprieve.

A few years later Oscar Langlois arrived at the station. If anyone deserved the title "Mr. Lighthouse of Oregon's South Coast," it was Langlois. Born at the Cape Blanco Lighthouse, where his father James was principal keeper, Langlois became an assistant keeper at Cape Arago in 1905. There he met and married Marie Amundsen, the principal keeper's daughter. The couple traveled to Coquille River, where Langlois served as assistant keeper before being promoted to principal keeper.

During their service at the station, Langlois and his assistant Charles Walters witnessed a fire that nearly destroyed Bandon. In September 1936, skies were filled with ashes and smoke as a forest fire swept into town, consuming 500 buildings and leaving only sixteen standing. The Langlois and Walters families provided food and shelter for some of the homeless. Meanwhile, the two keepers spent days cleaning up ashes and soot in the

13

tower and boiler room.

Langlois and Walters were the last keepers to serve at the Coquille River Lighthouse. In 1939 the Coast Guard decided the lighthouse was no longer needed and replaced it with an automated beacon at the end of the south jetty. Langlois retired, and he and Marie moved to the town of Coquille. Walters stayed on while equipment was removed from the lighthouse, then he was transferred to the Tillamook Rock Lighthouse. The dwelling was torn down, its lumber sold, and its roof tile installed on a Bandon home.

For twenty-four years the lighthouse stood abandoned until the creation of Bullards Beach State Park, which included the original eleven-acre lighthouse reservation. Park personnel tried to maintain the old lighthouse, but it was beyond simple repair. Walls were cracked; stucco and brick had fallen away. It required a major restoration.

This work began in 1976, with Oregon State Parks and the U.S. Army Corps of Engineers sharing the costs. The renovation was completed in 1979 and the lighthouse was reopened, with interpretive signs hanging in the old boiler room.

To celebrate Bandon's 1991 centennial, a new light was lit in the tower. This private, solar-powered light serves aesthetic purposes only and turns on at dusk and off at sunrise. Though no longer lit by keepers, the light's nightly glow reminds Bandon residents of the river's rich maritime past.

Directions and Hours: The entrance to Bullards Beach State Park is on the west side of Highway 101, just north of the Coquille River Bridge. Signs in the park show the way to the lighthouse. The lighthouse is open daily during daylight hours.

Chapter 3

Cape Arago Lighthouse

The Cape Arago light, south of the entrance to Coos Bay, stands on a small island near the cape. It shines from the third lighthouse built on the island, and is the state's oldest continuously operating light. Though not open to the public, the lighthouse can be seen from a spot near Sunset Bay State Park.

For centuries, Cape Arago was the home of Indians, who called the island "Chief's Island." Today it is covered by shell midden, and flowers planted by keepers' wives grow wild. Separated from the cape by a narrow, rock-filled channel, the island is shaped like a bony fist with an extended index finger pointing northward. Its steep sides, rising fifty feet above the water, are slowly crumbling into the sea.

The island's first lighthouse was built on the end of the finger-like point. Lit for the first time by principal keeper L. C. Hall on November 1, 1866, it became Oregon's second lighthouse.

The state's first lighthouse was built in 1857 near the mouth of the Umpqua River, twenty-five miles north of Coos Bay. At that time, the Umpqua was the busiest waterway on the south coast, but six years later, when the Umpqua River Lighthouse collapsed, Coos Bay had become a more important commercial center. Settlers had platted Empire City, and outbound vessels carried cargoes of lumber and coal to San Francisco. The Lighthouse Board reported that it was "of the opinion that the interests of commerce will be best subserved by establishing a new light upon Cape Arago, instead of re-erecting at Umpqua. . . . " Congress authorized funds for the Cape Arago light in 1864.

COAST GUARD MUSEUM NORTHWEST

Cape Arago's first lighthouse was built on the island's point in 1866.

The twenty-five-foot-high lighthouse on the island's point was an octagonal iron tower, supported by stilts. Inside the stilts, a staircase, exposed to wind and rain, circled up to a small watchroom and into the lantern room. There a rotating fourth-order Fresnel lens sent forth a beam of light visible for about fourteen miles.

On the island's lower end, a one-and-one-half-story wooden building was constructed to house the two lighthouse keepers. A 1,300-foot-long plank walkway with handrails connected the dwelling with the tower. Near the dwelling, a steeply inclined tramway lifted supplies from the beach.

Today it's an easy drive from Empire to Cape Arago. The highway crosses the bridge at South Slough and runs through Charleston and the woods to reach the homes, beaches, and parks on Cape Arago. For the early keepers, however, it was an arduous trip.

In 1870 C. W. Dickman, a Coos River homesteader, was assigned as assistant keeper. In Orvil Dodge's *Pioneer History of Coos and Curry Counties*, Dickman described his journey to the lighthouse. With his wife and baby, he rowed down the bay, past Empire City to the west side of South Slough, where they met a packer with horses. With Dickman on a horse, and his wife and baby on a pony, they pushed their way through thick woods and underbrush for about three miles to reach the lighthouse.

These difficulties, however, did not deter "a party of ladies and gentlemen of Empire City" from making an excursion to the lighthouse in the summer of 1874, as described in the *Coos Bay News*. The lively group of fourteen left Empire City in a large rowboat. At South Slough they pulled their boat ashore, walked through the woods, and were rowed across the narrow channel by keepers W. S. Roberts and Frank Langlois. After a sumptuous dinner, they stayed the night and in the morning "once more took of the bountiful hospitality of the 'Light-house Boys.'" The writer concluded, "Strong had been my desire to visit the lighthouse, but never had I conceived of the beauty and grandeur of the scenes presented to the eye, as I saw at Cape Arago."

An alternate route from the town to the lighthouse was to row or sail across the Coos Bay bar, then follow the coastline to the lighthouse. The route was seldom used, however, because it meant crossing hazardous waters. In the fall of 1881, assistant keeper William Walker went to Empire City to pick up a new station boat delivered from San Francisco. After

The second lighthouse and keepers' dwelling stood above an abandoned Life-Saving Service boathouse.

waiting for a favorable tide, Walker and a friend decided to take a shorter way past rocks and headlands rather than follow the channel across the bar. The boat capsized and both men drowned.

That same year a similar fate almost befell Thomas Brown as he tried to return to the island from South Slough. Brown was the keeper of the U.S. Life-Saving Service station on the island. He later told the *Coos Bay News* that, while crossing the bar in his fifteen-foot boat, he was blown northward. Unable to land in wind and rough seas, and with only a can of oysters, a beet, and a sack of onions, he sailed and rowed along the coast for three days. Finally, with his feet lashed to the seat, Brown got the boat ashore in heavy surf. He was north of Florence — nearly ninety miles from Cape Arago.

Two years after the experiences of Walker and Brown, overland access was improved with the completion of a wagon road from South Slough to the island. The road brought more sightseers, picnickers, and campers. They especially favored the beaches at Big Creek Bay, now called "Sunset Bay State Park."

Concerned about trespassers, the Lighthouse Service in 1886 extended a barbed-wire fence around the lighthouse reservation. This meant closing off the popular beach area. In a letter to keeper C. F. Smart, the district engineer issued strict orders: "The beach used by campers is . . . on the reservation and no one can be allowed to occupy it without authority." He then added, "Should I hear in the future that you allow such unauthorized occupation, I will recommend your discharge."

The *Coos Bay News* learned of the instructions to Smart and reported, "As the best camping places [are] at the mouth of Big Creek . . . this will be annoying to people in Coos and Douglas Counties, who desire to avail themselves of the sea breeze and a dip in the ocean during the hot weather." Nevertheless, the barbed-wire fence was completed. After a year of listening to complaints, however, the Lighthouse Service allowed the campers to return the following summer.

Vacationers weren't Cape Arago's only visitors. In December of 1891, the ship *General Butler* sank about 100 miles southwest of the cape. Keeper Frank Carlson was surprised when the survivors came ashore at the lighthouse station. "They were in an almost exhausted condition having been in the boat for four days without anything to eat or drink," wrote Carlson. He and assistant Thomas Wyman took care of the men, and the next day escorted them to Empire City.

One long-standing problem for the keepers was how to get from the mainland to the island. A low footbridge, built across the channel in 1876, proved costly to maintain. It was washed away twice and was in constant need of repair. In 1889 the Lighthouse Service decided to build a high bridge. Bids for its construction were exorbitant, however, and a 400-foot-long tramway with a cable car was built instead. The car, suspended about sixty feet above the water, was pulled across the channel by a hand-operated winch on the island.

Completed in 1891, the cable car system worked well for about seven years. Then the Lighthouse Service decided to build the high bridge and ordered materials delivered to the station. As the bridge neared completion, a terrible accident occurred. According to Stephen Dow Beckman in the *Coos Historical Quarterly*, keeper Thomas Wyman, one of his daughters, and two others were being winched across the inlet. The cable broke, and they plunged to the water below. Wyman's legs were crushed. The tender *Columbine*, at the station with a cargo of supplies, picked up the injured and took them to Empire City. One of Wyman's legs had to be amputated. Eight weeks later the bridge (still in use today) was completed.

Another problem was the fog, which became more of a hazard as vessel traffic increased. The district engineer reported that "the commerce of these waters would be greatly benefited by placing a first-class fog signal on the point of the island. . . . " In 1896 a Daboll trumpet was installed in a brick building next to the light tower. Other improvements were made: the tower was also enclosed in brick, and a new dwelling for three keepers was built.

The fog signal had been operating barely ten years when erosion on the point began to undermine the fog signal building and the light tower. At the same time, ships' captains were complaining that the signals were antiquated and should be replaced by modern equipment.

The Lighthouse Service agreed and built a wood-frame fog signal building with an attached tower on the lower end of the island. With this new, higher tower, the light was 100 feet above the water instead of seventy-five feet, as it had been previously. This made the light visible for sixteen miles instead of fourteen. The new light and the siren fog signal began operation on July 1, 1909.

Construction of the third Cape Arago tower began in the early 1930s. Local resident R. J. "Rudy" Hillstrom was awarded the contract, which included razing the first tower. "People could visit the lighthouse then," said Thomas Hillstrom, Rudy's son. "They'd come to see the second lighthouse and wander out on the narrow ridge to see the original light-house. It was dangerous, so the Lighthouse Service decided to blow it up." All that remains of the first lighthouse is the center rod of the tower's staircase and a few bricks.

Hillstrom built the third lighthouse from plans used to build Washington's Point Robinson Lighthouse. The concrete building housed a new fog sig-nal, and the attached, two-story octagonal tower held a fourth-order Fresnel

TONY HOSTETTER

Cape Arago's third lighthouse now stands alone on the island.

lens. It began operation in 1934. The second lighthouse, with its tower removed, served as the keepers' office.

The Cape Arago Lighthouse was automated in 1966. Eventually all the island's buildings except the lighthouse were razed. In the spring and summer of 1993, the lighthouse was renovated. Coast guardsmen carried scaffolding, tools, paint, and cement by hand across the bridge. They power-washed the lighthouse with water from the cisterns, and painted the tower and fog signal building a gleaming white.

The fourth-order Fresnel lens, which rotated on a bed of mercury, was removed later. The Coast Guard was concerned that an earthquake might spill the mercury or that the old bridge would collapse in a storm, making it difficult to retrieve the lens. At 10 A.M. on September 20, 1993, the light in the old lens was switched off, and a light in a modern optic was turned on.

The lens is being stored by the Coast Guard, but will be displayed again someday. The Confederated Tribes of Coos, Lower Umpqua, and Siuslaw Indians, in partnership with the Bureau of Land Management and the Coast Guard, are planning a major interpretive center on the mainland opposite the island. One idea is to place the lens in a tower at the center. Perhaps, someday, Cape Arago's light will shine from a fourth tower.

Directions and Hours: The lighthouse can be seen from a turnout on the south side of Sunset Bay State Park, about twelve miles west of Highway 101. From Coos Bay or North Bend, follow signs marked "Charleston" and "Ocean Beaches." Past Charleston, follow signs for Sunset Bay Beach.

Chapter 4

Umpqua River Lighthouse

The 100-year-old Umpqua River Lighthouse, its first-order Fresnel lens flashing red and white, is the second lighthouse to mark the river's mouth. The first, built in 1857, stood for only six years before falling victim to the river's floods.

The Umpqua River heads in the Cascades, then takes a gentle course to the sea. It flows through a broad interior valley, narrower Coast Range valleys, and between forested slopes before tumbling to the head of tidewater.

Those were the observations of a group of San Francisco land investors who came north on the vessel *Samuel Roberts* in the spring of 1850. They crossed the bar and sailed thirty miles to the head of tidewater, where Levi Scott and others were settling what would become Scottsburg. The investors secured lots at the settlement and established claims farther upriver.

Returning to San Francisco, the investors promoted their findings. A September 1850 ad in the *Oregon Spectator* cited the Umpqua River Valley as "fine fertile country, (now rapidly filling up)." It described the town being laid out at Scottsburg and its "delightfully located" harbor. It failed to mention the hazards of the Umpqua River's bar.

Less than a month later, these hazards became apparent when the vessel *Bostonian* foundered at the river's mouth. Soon after, the vessel *Kate Heath* arrived from San Francisco with new settlers and merchandise. It crossed the bar safely, but at a high cost. Five men from the wrecked

TED NELSON

The second Umpqua River Lighthouse was built on a ridge after floods destroyed the first lighthouse.

Bostonian, who came to assist the crossing, were drowned when their small boat capsized.

Despite the river's dangerous bar, Scottsburg became the port of entry for goods and settlers bound for the Umpqua's valleys and for miners headed to the mines of southwest Oregon and northern California.

At the same time, the Coast Survey was selecting sites for the West Coast's first lighthouses. One of the first sixteen sites chosen was at the Umpqua River's mouth. An initial appropriation for the light was authorized by Congress in August 1852. A strong supporter of the lighthouse was Joseph Lane who, as Territorial Governor, served as a delegate to Congress. (Lane also held a land claim in the Umpqua Valley.) More funds were appropriated in 1854, but construction was delayed as priority was given to lighthouses elsewhere.

Construction finally began in 1855 when materials were delivered by ship from San Francisco. The site selected was on the river's sandy north spit. The lighthouse's design was similar to many other early West Coast lighthouses. The Cape Cod-style dwelling had keepers' quarters on each side of the nearly ninety-two-foot-high tower, which extended through the center of the building's gabled roof. A narrow spiral staircase led from the first floor to the lantern room atop the tower.

Hindered by the region's stormy weather, construction went slowly. It wasn't until October 10, 1857, that keeper Fayette Crosby, a former hotel keeper in Scottsburg, first lit the lamp in the third-order Fresnel lens. In spite of the delays, however, the Umpqua River Lighthouse was the first on the Oregon Coast. Oregon itself would not gain statehood for another two years.

The site selected for this first lighthouse was ill-fated. Close to the Umpqua's edge, the lighthouse suffered from the river's frequent flooding — a problem that led to the station's eventual destruction.

A flood that destroyed much of Scottsburg on February 8, 1861 is often blamed for the demise of the lighthouse. However, the official Light Lists show that the lighthouse continued operation into 1863. During a severe storm that October, the foundation was washed away to the extent that it was feared that the next storm would destroy the structure. The lens was removed, and according to the Lighthouse Board report of 1864, "While the workmen were engaged in taking down the lantern, . . . the tower began to exhibit symptoms of tottering, and soon afterwards fell."

COAST GUARD MUSEUM NORTHWEST

Workers celebrate the near-completion of the second tower in 1892.

The *Oregon Statesman* for February 29, 1864, printed the station's epitaph: " . . . The lighthouse, at the mouth of the Umpqua River fell about three weeks ago, from being gradually undermined by the action of the water on its sandy foundation."

It was over thirty years before the Umpqua River was again graced with a lighthouse. Even as the first lighthouse was being built, Scottsburg was losing its importance as a port of entry. New land laws had squashed the hopes of the early land investors; Coos Bay was becoming a major shipping center; and California's Crescent City became the favored port of entry to Oregon's southwest interior.

Nevertheless, the Umpqua River saw many ships during its unlighted years. Produce from the fertile valleys was shipped across the bar, and ships were built along the river's lower shores. Salmon-canning and sawmilling flourished in the 1870s.

But it wasn't until 1888 that Congress and the Lighthouse Board again turned their attention to the Umpqua. In that year funds were appropriated for a primary seacoast light at the river's mouth.

The Lighthouse Board's objective was to establish lighthouses so that mariners would enter the visible range of one light as they passed from the range of another. At this time, the nearest lighthouse to the Umpqua was twenty-five miles to the south at Cape Arago, a secondary light with a range of only about fourteen miles. The Yaquina Head light to the north had a range of nineteen miles, but it was seventy-three miles away. Thus, funds were authorized for primary seacoast lights at Heceta Head and at the Umpqua River. The addition of these two lights, each with a range of about twenty miles, would close an unlighted gap along Oregon's coast.

The site selected for the Umpqua's second lighthouse was safely above the river, on a 100-foot-high ridge overlooking the sand dunes on the river's south side. Plans for the new lighthouse were completed and construction bids opened in April 1891.

A satisfactory bid was received for the metal work, including the lantern, lantern roof, gallery, and tower stairs. These items were delivered to the site on the tender *Manzanita* in March 1892.

But many obstacles still stood in the way of the second lighthouse's completion. The bids received to build the two keepers' dwellings and the tower exceeded the funds available. New bids were received in the fall of 1891, and work was well underway in early 1892. Then the dwelling contractor became bankrupt and stopped work. That part of the project had to be bid again.

In January 1893 all that remained to be done was install the illuminating apparatus and the lens. In this final step of construction, the lens' base was found to be fifteen inches short. All the appropriated funds had been spent, and a watchman was placed in charge of the station until Congress authorized more money.

Funds were finally obtained in August 1894, and on December 31 keeper Marinus Stream cranked the clockwork mechanism that turned the first-order Fresnel lens. He lit the lamp, and once again a light beamed across the Umpqua River's bar. Red panels mounted on the lens created a light that flashed white twice, then once red, every fifteen seconds.

The station's first two years were marred by tragedy. In November

1895 the steamer *Bandorilla* foundered on the bar when its tiller rope gave way. Just one year earlier, this vessel had brought keeper Stream's family to the station from Astoria. As the ship came broadside in the breakers, the captain was washed overboard and drowned. Stream and his first assistant, Isaac Smith, recovered the body.

On August 14, 1896, Stream's entry in the log, written in his bold script, reported: "General duties. Light S.W. Cloudy." The next entry that same day, written in a finer hand, reads: "Mr M. A. Stream, the keeper of this station, was drowned today at 1:30 P.M."

Despite its unhappy beginning, the station later became a favorite with Lighthouse Service personnel and the coast guardsmen who followed. Except for a brief outage caused by a fire in 1958, the light's unique red and white characteristic faithfully guided mariners for eighty-nine years.

Then, in November 1983, the lens' chariot wheel mechanism failed. This mechanism, which supported the heavy lens and guided its turning, had caused trouble before. The Coast Guard installed a temporary rotating beacon on the tower and proposed that the beacon permanently replace the classical lens. A howl of protest came from local residents, who wanted to keep the authentic lens in use.

The Coast Guard relented. With the help of Brass Connections, a Reedsport firm, and a Kirkland, Washington, company, the load-bearing guide wheels and guide rings were rebuilt using modern technology. The lens went back into service on January 14, 1985.

Visitors to the Umpqua River Lighthouse can see the gleaming white tower, its attached workroom, and its revolving red and white lens. Newer Coast Guard buildings have replaced the original wood-frame keepers' dwellings. Entry to the lighthouse grounds is not currently allowed, but future plans call for public access to the workroom.

Nearby, the Douglas County Parks Department maintains a historical and information center in an old Coast Guard building. In the spring of 1994, the Lower Umpqua Chamber of Commerce in Reedsport was planning an August celebration to mark the second lighthouse's 100th year.

A viewing platform near the lighthouse is one of the best places on the coast to watch the interaction of wind, wave, and river flow that marks a river's bar. Though the bar is now tamed by jetties and dredging, one can sense the powerful forces encountered by Oregon's early mariners, and the importance of the lighthouses that guided them on their way.

Directions and Hours: The lighthouse, about one mile west of Highway 101, is in Umpqua Lighthouse State Park about six miles south of Reedsport. Turn at the park sign and follow the lighthouse signs, staying to the right at the overnight camping area. The park is open daily. The historical and information center is open from May 1 to September 30. Wednesday through Saturday hours are 10:00 A.M. to 5:00 P.M. Sunday hours are 1:00 P.M. to 5:00 P.M.

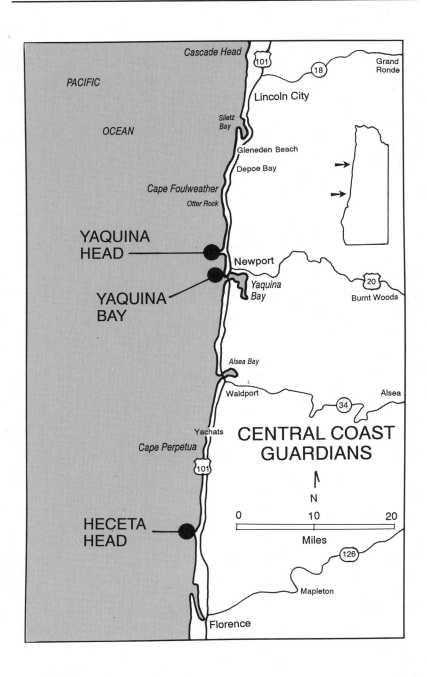

Section 2

Central Coast Guardians

European explorers began to return to the Pacific Northwest in 1774. They had been absent for 170 years while their nations fought wars, consolidated territories, and pursued trade with Asia by sending ships east around Africa's Cape of Good Hope.

The first to return were the Spanish, coming north from Mexico to counter Russian incursions down the icy coast of Alaska and to resume the search for the Northwest Passage.

In 1778 Captain James Cook, searching for the Northwest Passage on behalf of England, reached the Oregon Coast near Yaquina Bay. Though blown about by gales, he named capes Foulweather and Perpetua before sailing on in a vain search for the passage.

At Nootka Sound, on today's Vancouver Island, Cook's men traded bits of metal to Indians for sea otter pelts. Later, Chinese merchants in Macao bought these pelts for up to $100 each. Word of the potential wealth in the maritime fur trade spread along the world's shipping lanes. English traders began coming to the Northwest in 1776. American traders soon followed.

The central Oregon Coast was outside the mainstream of the maritime fur trade and the influx of settlers to the South Coast in the 1850s. By the 1870s, however, Yaquina Bay was becoming a lumber, shipbuilding, and oyster-shipping center.

A harbor light was established at the bay's entrance in 1871, and seacoast lights were later established at Yaquina Head and Heceta Head. The latter two are still in operation, and the Yaquina Bay Lighthouse is a museum.

TED NELSON

Heceta Head's lighthouse still has its original Fresnel lens.

Chapter 5

Heceta Head Lighthouse

High above sea-washed rocks, a light flashes twenty-four hours a day from Heceta Head's tower. A short distance away, a white dwelling, its roof painted red, stands bright against a dark forest. This is the scene travelers driving north on Highway 101 see of the century-old lighthouse station.

Heceta Head, named for Spanish explorer Don Bruno de Heceta, was selected as a lighthouse site to fill an unlighted gap on the Oregon Coast between Yaquina Head's light and one to be built on the Umpqua River. An appropriation of $80,000 was made in 1889 for site purchase and construction. The Lighthouse Service then selected, surveyed, and bought the site, and staked out a wagon road.

The road to Florence, about twelve miles to the south, was first on the construction list for good reason. Lumber and pipe could arrive by water from Florence, but other supplies, including bricks, cement, and explosives, had to be hauled overland. One thousand barrels of powder were used to level benches for the tower and the two keepers' dwellings. The deafening noise sent birds and deer fleeing, but one reporter wrote that "Blasting at the lighthouse does not seem to scare the sea lions away."

According to Stephanie Finucane in *Heceta House: A Historical and Architectural Survey*, when construction was in full swing, fifty-six men were working on the station: carpenters, laborers, teamsters, a bookkeeper, and a foreman. Some lived in tents. Others boarded with Dolly and Welcome Warren. The Warrens, homesteading 160 acres at Heceta Head, had sold the government nineteen acres of land for the lighthouse reservation.

By January 1893, the construction crew had completed two oil houses, a barn, and two Queen Anne-style dwellings, a single home for the principal keeper and a duplex for the assistants. Winter storms delayed work on the tower, but it was finished in August. The first-order Fresnel lens and its clockwork turning mechanism arrived in crates aboard the tender *Manzanita* and were brought ashore in a surfboat. By December the lens was installed in the fifty-six-foot-tall tower, but it remained dark until its lamp arrived from New York. It was delivered in February, and finally lit March 30, 1894. The light, 205 feet above the sea, flashed white for eight seconds every minute and was visible for twenty-one miles.

Andrew Hald, the first principal keeper at Heceta Head, had served at Cape Meares when it was first lit four years earlier. His first assistants were Eugene Walters and John Cowan. By 1896 Hald had seen seven assistant keepers come and go — including Cowen and J. Frank Barker, who were promoted and transferred to start up the new Coquille River station.

Coming and going to Heceta Head was difficult during the lighthouse's early years. The wagon road to Florence climbed steeply up Sea Lion Point to the south, and was impassable much of the year. Vessels could anchor near the lighthouse only in calm seas.

Because of its remoteness, Heceta Head had a post office to serve the keepers and neighboring ranchers, though deliveries were sporadic. The little community also had a school district with a one-room schoolhouse. Keepers and their families tended large vegetable gardens and raised chickens and cows. Hunting and fishing trips brought variety to the menu, as venison, trout, or salmon graced the dinner table.

Olaf Hansen became principal keeper in 1904. This was Hansen's second assignment at Heceta Head. While he was assistant keeper from 1896 to 1902, he and his wife Annie began a family that grew to include five girls and a boy.

After an assignment at a Washington lighthouse, Hansen was happy to return and join his family; Annie and their children had stayed behind, tending their homestead near Florence. In addition to his keeper's duties, Hansen was the postmaster and a member of the school board.

A larger one-room schoolhouse was built about 1916 near the north end of the present highway bridge, close to Cape Creek. One teacher taught

Heceta Head's keepers, their families, and the school teacher pose for a picture. Principal keeper Olaf Hansen is on the right in the back row. Circa 1913.

all eight grades. Of the fourteen children attending the school, nine were keepers' children, and six of those nine were Hansens.

The Hansen family left in 1920 when Olaf was transferred to Willapa Bay Lighthouse in Washington. Frank DeRoy, who had earlier served at Heceta Head, arrived with his wife Jenny and son Bob from Washington's Lime Kiln Lighthouse to replace Hansen.

Bob was five years old when he began to attend the school. "In class when we happened to see salmon going upstream, as we could see them from the windows, we would just run out and fish," he recalled later. Bob also fished with his father, but neither hunted. "Dad couldn't even kill a chicken for dinner."

As Bob grew older, he often helped his father with lighthouse chores: "I was fascinated by the workings in the lighthouse. Dad and I shined all the brass fittings, made things tidy and neat, like he was expecting the inspector any minute."

Each day the keepers washed the glass panes of the lantern, cleaned the lens, and polished the lamp and clockwork. Their wives and children kept the homes swept, the contents of drawers neat, and the brass dustpan gleaming. That way, on "boat day" when the tender dropped anchor, if the inspector's flag was flying from the mast to announce his arrival, the family was ready.

"Everyone happily anticipated 'boat day,'" said Bob. The tender would bring food, lighthouse supplies, mail, and packages from catalog orders. "Boat day" occurred three or four times a year. If the keepers needed store-bought supplies in the intervening months, neighbor Charles Stonefield hitched his two Clydesdales to a wagon to travel to Florence. It took him two days to make the round trip. DeRoy chose another way: "Dad traveled to Florence on foot in good weather to get needed supplies, which he carried in a pack on his back."

The DeRoys left Heceta Head in 1925 and were replaced by Clifford B. Hermann, who had started with the Lighthouse Service in 1905. He and his wife, Annie, had lived at Tatoosh Island (Cape Flattery) and Destruction Island, both off-shore light stations in Washington. While at Heceta Head, Hermann would see many changes, including an end to its isolation.

When Hermann arrived, the only unfinished part of the Oregon Coast Highway was between Yachats and Florence. A road did connect the towns, but it was narrow, muddy, and infrequently used, except by mail carriers who rode horseback. In 1926, according to Finucane, a new carrier used his 1918 Model-T Ford, with thirteen forward and eight reverse gears, but still got stuck in the mud.

In 1930 crews arrived to build the highway. They brought their wives and children, and set up tents and makeshift cabins on the beach below the station at Cape Creek. Hermann, observing the scene, told a reporter that he was "virtually surrounded by road builders and the day of lonesomeness has passed."

When work was completed in 1932, a bridge spanned Cape Creek, and a tunnel led through the hillside toward Sea Lion Point.

In 1934 electricity came to the station. An electric motor now turned the lens, and a light bulb replaced the lamp. Eventually the second assistant keeper's position was eliminated. The Hermanns moved into the duplex, and in 1940 the single dwelling was torn down.

Heceta Head circa 1932. The newly completed Coast Highway can be seen above the dwellings.

During World War II, Hermann, who continued as a civilian keeper under the Coast Guard, was again "virtually surrounded," this time by coast guardsmen. Fearing Japanese attacks, the Coast Guard assigned large numbers of personnel to lighthouse stations along the coast. Seventy-five men moved into a barracks and ate in a mess hall built where the single dwelling had stood. With dogs at their sides, they patrolled the beaches from near Florence to Yachats. A look-out tower was built above the lighthouse.

With the war's end, quiet came once again. After serving for forty-nine years as a lighthouse keeper, Hermann retired in January 1950 at age seventy.

The last keeper was Oswald Allik, who came to Heceta Head in 1957 after he turned out the light at the Tillamook Rock Lighthouse for the last time. Life at Heceta Head was easier. There were no more drenching waves to battle, no fog signal to tend. Each evening he sat down to dinner with his wife, instead of eating in silence with three keepers.

On July 20, 1963, Allik turned the switch that automated Heceta Head's light. He retired the same day.

Until the government decided what to do with the station, personnel from Oregon State Parks and the U.S. Forest Service rented the dwelling. Eventually the Forest Service acquired the property, except for two acres retained by the Coast Guard where the lighthouse and oil houses stood. The Forest Service lacked the funds to keep the dwelling in good repair, and it continued to deteriorate.

In 1970, Lane County Community College leased the dwelling for use as classrooms. In exchange for rent, the college agreed to hire caretakers and to do interior repairs. None of the caretakers lasted long until Harry and Anne Tammen arrived in 1973.

During the Tammens' sixteen-year stay, they witnessed major changes to the dwelling. It was listed on the National Historic Register in 1978. Funding for restoration was secured. A wire fence around the dwelling was replaced by a picket fence, similar to the original. The leaky roof was replaced, and the porch was reconstructed to include replicas of the wood spindles used in the balustrade. The work took four years, and the dwelling now appears as it did when the first keepers moved in.

In the early 1990s the Coast Guard began restoring Oregon's lighthouse towers in preparation to turn them over to local groups or government agencies. The Coast Guard will continue to maintain the lights and fog signals, while the group or agency will maintain the structures and in some cases improve public access. Under this plan, Heceta Head's lighthouse was restored in the summer of 1993.

The college continues to hold classes in the dwelling, and caretakers no longer worry about a leaky roof. The dwelling, tower, and two nearby oil houses are not open to the public, but visitors can park at Devils Elbow State Park on the beach and hike up a trail for a pleasant view of the lighthouse. In the spring of 1994, the Forest Service, the State of Oregon, and the Coast Guard were discussing future plans for the lighthouse. One day, instead of just admiring it from the outside, visitors may get an inside look at Heceta Head's dwelling and the tower's workroom.

Directions and Hours: The road to Devils Elbow State Park is west of Highway 101, near Milepost 178. The road's entrance is signed. The park is open daily during daylight hours. For current access information, phone the U.S. Forest Service office at Waldport: (503) 563-3211.

TED NELSON

Yaquina Bay's lighthouse, once destined for demolition, was saved and is now popular with visitors.

Chapter 6

Yaquina Bay Lighthouse

On a pine-covered hill near Newport, at the mouth of the Yaquina River, stands the 1871 Yaquina Bay Lighthouse. A favorite with visitors, few would guess that its light shone for only three years, and it was once scheduled for demolition.

Five years before the lighthouse was built, David Newsome, an influential Willamette Valley agriculturist, came to Yaquina Bay to investigate its commercial opportunities. The area, once an Indian reservation, had recently been opened to settlement.

The report of his trip, a glowing assessment of the bay's potential, was sent to the state's congressional delegation. "1,000 vessels can be anchored in it [the bay] in safety," reported Newsome. "Its entrance is superior to any inlet from San Francisco to Puget Sound." If a transcontinental railroad terminated at the bay, Newsome said, "a city, like that of San Francisco, would arise."

By 1868 a railroad was still in the future, but a wagon road connected Corvallis with the bay. Lumber schooners, sailing from the bay's first sawmill, joined oyster schooners on their way to San Francisco.

Two years later Congress concluded that a lighthouse was needed on the bay, and funding was authorized. The Lighthouse Board announced that construction would begin as soon as a suitable site could be obtained.

This action was taken despite the advice of Colonel R. S. Stockton, the Lighthouse Service district engineer. He said that a first-order light should be built on Cape Foulweather (Yaquina Head) instead of a harbor light on the bay.

The abandoned Yaquina Bay Lighthouse as it looked in the 1890s.

Nevertheless, a site was selected on thirty-six acres at the bay's sandy north head. It was purchased from pioneers Lester and Sophrina Baldwin for $500 in gold coin. Construction began in May 1871.

The work went quickly, and by the end of October 1871 the new station was complete. The sturdily built wood-frame building had two stories and a basement. Chimneys stood near each end of the gabled roof. A three-story tower rose from the rear of the building, its lantern housing a small, fifth-order Fresnel lens.

A half hour before sunset on November 3, 1871, the station's first and only keeper, Charles H. Peirce (pronounced *Purse*), lit the whale oil lamp in the fixed lens. The new light joined Cape Blanco, Cape Arago, and Cape Disappointment as one of four lighthouses guiding mariners along Oregon's waters.

Keeper Peirce had moved into the lighthouse with his wife, Sarah, and six of their children, who ranged in age from two to eighteen. Another child would be born at the lighthouse later. Peirce had served as a captain in the Union Army, and is said by descendants to have been a friend of Ulysses S. Grant.

Even before Yaquina Bay's lamp was lit, however, the Lighthouse Board had reconsidered Colonel Stockton's advice. It decided that a light was needed on Yaquina Head, and in August 1873 a first-order light went into operation there.

The new seacoast light had a range of nineteen miles, which the Lighthouse Board deemed satisfactory to meet the needs of mariners in the area. The Yaquina Bay light was ordered discontinued. Peirce and his family packed their belongings for a move to Cape Blanco's lighthouse. He extinguished the Yaquina Bay light for the last time on October 1, 1874.

Though occasionally occupied by caretakers, the lighthouse, with its lens removed, began to fall into disrepair. In 1877 the station was put up for sale, but the price offered was too low and the offer was withdrawn. A year later the structure was described as almost uninhabitable. The roof and outside sheathing had to be renewed to prevent the building from completely falling apart.

There was some talk that the light might be reactivated when a railroad arrived. Colonel T. Egerton Hogg dreamed of building a railroad from Corvallis to the bay, as the agriculturalist Newsome had envisioned. In 1880 Hogg organized the Oregon Pacific Railroad Company, and in March 1885 the first train arrived from Corvallis. Willamette Valley produce joined the cargoes of oysters, lumber, and fish leaving the bay.

Regular passenger service between San Francisco and the bay on the steamship *Yaquina City* was inaugurated in connection with the railroad. In December 1877 the ship was wrecked as it crossed the bar. A year later the replacement vessel *Yaquina Bay* met the same fate.

Although the passengers and crews were saved and both wrecks had been caused by mechanical failure, the losses diminished the port's stature. The lighthouse was not reactivated. Small, unmanned lanterns were added later to assist nighttime bar crossings, and the old lighthouse became officially listed only as a "day beacon."

This period saw the beginning of a long line of tenants for the structure. Starting in 1888, the U.S. Army Corps of Engineers quartered personnel there while the river's jetties were being constructed. In 1906 the Yaquina Bay Life-Saving Service moved into the old lighthouse and used the tower as a lookout until 1933. A modern Coast Guard lookout tower now stands nearby.

A year later the lighthouse and its surrounding property was acquired by the state as a park. Park and highway personnel then occupied the building. In 1946 the Oregon State Highway Commission, unwilling to spend money for necessary repairs, decided the building should be demolished.

But by then the old lighthouse had become deeply woven into the fabric of the Newport community. The lighthouse was the area's oldest building, and had been immortalized by Lischen M. Miller's short story, "The Haunted Light at Newport By The Sea." Published in 1899, this story told of a sea captain's daughter who disappeared in the abandoned lighthouse.

Now the people of Newport rallied to save their "haunted" lighthouse, but according to James M. Howes, writing for the Lincoln County Historical Society, the effort seemed hopeless. Howes recounts the unsuccessful search for private donations and the failure of five successive tax measures. Time was running out. With a wrecking crew reportedly on the way, a farewell party was held. Then the highway commission relented, making more time available. Another campaign was launched, without tangible results.

In 1955 the highway commission changed its stand and committed a small amount of funds to stop the decay of the old lighthouse. A year later, a ceremony was held to dedicate the lighthouse as a significant historical landmark. It then was leased to the Lincoln County Historical Society as a museum.

Beginning in 1974, state park crews fully restored the building and furnished it with authentic 1870 pieces on loan from the Oregon Historical Society. Today the lighthouse is open regularly to the public under the aegis of the Friends of Yaquina Bay Lighthouse, Inc.

Paul Kuper, president of the "Friends," proudly shows visitors the fine craftsmanship that went into the lighthouse. Joists are secured with wooden pegs. There are no cracks in the brick floor laid on a bed of sand, and the roof's gutters are of hand-carved redwood, glued with pitch.

Kuper proudly says that, on some summer days, the lighthouse has as many as 400 visitors. The "Friends" now have members throughout the nation. Such support is rare for a lighthouse, especially for one whose light shone for only three years.

Directions and Hours: From the north, on Highway 101, turn right at the sign for Yaquina Bay State Park and Historic Lighthouse, at the north end of the Yaquina Bay Bridge. From the south, turn right at the Coast Guard sign immediately after crossing the bridge, then turn under the bridge. The lighthouse is open daily, Memorial Day to September 30, from 11:00 A.M. to 5:00 P.M. In other months, it is open Saturdays and Sundays from noon to 4:00 P.M. Weddings and group tours can be arranged. Phone: (503) 862-7451.

TED NELSON

Yaquina Head's 1873 seacoast tower was refurbished by the U.S. Coast Guard in 1993.

Chapter 7

Yaquina Head Lighthouse

The Yaquina Head Lighthouse is a classical seacoast tower, the tallest on the Oregon Coast. It stands on a low, narrow peninsula about three miles north of Newport. Completed in 1873, its first-order Fresnel lens still shines from the ninety-three-foot tower. Like the peninsula that is so often enveloped in fog, the lighthouse has been shrouded in the myth that it was built in the wrong place.

The myth about the station's location was fostered by the book *Oregon*, published in 1940 as one of the American Guide Book Series compiled by the Works Projects Administration. The book stated that the lighthouse "was to have been placed on Otter Crest but construction materials were delivered here [Yaquina Head] by mistake." Otter Crest was a name sometimes given to Cape Foulweather, seven miles to the north of Yaquina Head.

Initially, the misconception was caused by the Lighthouse Board. In its early reports it referred to the light as being at Cape Foulweather. Research by historian Stephen Dow Beckham, however, led him to conclude that "The engineers knew precisely what they were doing [in placing the lighthouse at Yaquina Head] and did so on the basis of careful study and calculation."

Beckham's findings are confirmed by General Land Office records and survey plats completed in the early days of the lighthouse. They describe the true location of the lighthouse, but the head now known as Yaquina is titled "Cape Foulweather." It was a case of a confusion of names, not a confusion of places. Correction of the myth is gradually being made in lighthouse literature.

OREGON HISTORICAL SOCIETY-25533

This original keepers' dwelling and later buildings are now gone.

Congress appropriated funds for the light station in March 1871. The plans for the tower were adapted from California's Pigeon Point Lighthouse. Construction began in the fall of 1871, forcing builders to battle winter storms. Two boats were lost in rough seas while trying to land building materials at the site. The schooner bringing construction supplies from San Francisco usually had to off-load at Newport, with the materials shipped to the head by wagon over a torturous road.

Gradually the light station took shape. The lantern and lens arrived in the spring of 1872. Sections of the lens, built in France, were packed in separate crates, transhipped through New York, and portaged across Panama. Over 370,000 bricks were delivered from San Francisco and laid into the double-walled tower. The keeper's dwelling, a two-and-one-half-story wooden building with a basement, was finished in October.

Almost all was ready for an early 1873 lighting when it was discovered that a piece of the lantern had been lost in transit. The lighting was delayed while a replacement piece was fabricated.

On August 20, 1873, keeper Fayette Crosby crossed the marbled lower floor of the tower. He climbed the 114 stairs to the lantern room and lit Yaquina Head's lamp for the first time. It was not a new experience for Crosby, who in 1857 had been the first to light the lamp in Oregon's first lighthouse at the Umpqua River.

Though there was no fog signal to operate, the station was usually manned by three keepers. The principal keeper, the first assistant, and their families shared the main dwelling. In the early days of the station, the second assistant keeper was relegated to sleeping in the workshop.

The weather that impeded the station's construction continued to batter the station after it was built. Wind-driven rain leaked into the keepers' dwelling, making it necessary to add more siding. In 1879 a March storm blew down a long section of picket fence and ripped shingles from the dwelling's roof. Small rocks, torn from the cliff by the wind, shattered windows. In 1880 a high fence was built along the cliff's edge to intercept them. It successfully shielded the building from the rocks, but ocean spray continued to strike the dwelling in severe storms.

Lightning was also a hazard. In October 1920 it struck the tower while assistant keeper Wilson Auld was in the watchroom beneath the lantern. The whole tower jarred. Auld hurried down the stairs and at first noticed nothing unusual. In the hall between the tower and the workroom, he found that a piece of ceiling molding had been torn loose and rain was pouring through the hole. Returning to the tower later, he saw that on each handrail newel post except the bottom one, the black paint had been burned away, exposing the red lead paint beneath.

On the flat, treeless point the principal keepers, their assistants, and their families created a small community. The station's early residents relied on supplies delivered by the lighthouse tender. They also gathered vegetables from a large garden, pastured cows, raised chickens, and occasionally went to Newport for other supplies. These trips were made along a plank road that the keepers helped maintain.

Like any community, Yaquina Head saw life and death. In the 1920s William Smith was the principal keeper. One evening he loaded his family into the wagon for a trip to Newport. Before Smith left, assistant keeper Frank Story agreed to light the lamps for Herbert Higgins, the other assistant, who was ill. On arriving at Newport, Smith looked back and saw that the tower was dark. He quickly loaded his family into the wagon and hurried back to the station.

According to his granddaughter, Virginia (Smith) Winfolk, keeper Smith discovered that Story, having had a few too many to drink, had failed to go up in the tower. Higgins was not in his quarters. When Smith went upstairs, he found Higgins lying on the landing in the tower. Higgins had tried to light the lamp despite his illness. He died in the tower. Thereafter, assistant Story, filled with guilt, would enter the tower only when accompanied by a bulldog to protect him from Higgins' ghost.

Another assistant keeper at Yaquina Head was Fred Booth. His daughter Marguerite was born at the station in June 1916. She recalls her mother telling how the dwelling shook during storms. Sometimes, after a particularly harsh storm, the family feasted on ducks and geese that had broken their necks flying into the lantern. Mrs. Booth often entertained other keepers and friends from Newport, playing the piano and guitar. Though Fred Booth liked lighthouse work, his wife disliked the fog, so the family moved in 1918.

That year, a Signal Corps squadron was camped near the head. The troops were logging spruce trees to build World War I airplanes. According to historian Beckham, the officers of the squadron petitioned the Lighthouse Service to allow the troops to visit the station. The request was denied because "they [the squadron personnel] are not on official business and it would be impractical to make such distinctions in admitting visitors."

The restrictions were lifted after the war, and in 1924 the keepers reported nearly 10,000 visitors. A year later, regular visitor hours were posted. In 1938, with over twelve thousand visitors, Yaquina Head was the most visited lighthouse on the West Coast and fourth most visited in the nation. The Lighthouse Service reported that during visiting hours it became necessary to station one keeper in the tower and one below to admit groups of suitable size.

Electricity reached the head in the early 1930s, and the light's characteristic was changed from fixed to flashing. In 1938 the original dwelling and another built later were replaced by a smaller building used by Coast

Guard personnel. The newer building was later demolished, leaving only the tower and adjoining workroom standing.

Despite the lighthouse's popularity with visitors, the Coast Guard closed the tower to the public for many years. In 1993 the tower, refurbished and painted by the Coast Guard, was turned over to the Bureau of Land Management to be part of the Yaquina Head Outstanding Natural Area.

The light will continue to be maintained by the Coast Guard, but the tower will once again be open to visitors beginning in June 1994. There will be tours to the watchroom for small groups on a first-come-first-served basis. Be sure to arrive early: the newly established natural area is already receiving over 400,000 visitors every year.

Directions and Hours: The Yaquina Head Outstanding Natural Area is well signed and is located about three miles north of Newport on Highway 101. The natural area is open all year from dawn to dusk. In 1994, from June 1 to September 15, the lower floor of the tower will be open every day from 11:00 A.M. to 3:00 P.M. Watchroom tours will run daily every half-hour from 9:00 A.M. to 11:00 A.M., and 3:00 P.M. to 4:00 P.M. They are on a first-come-first-served basis, and are limited to fifteen people. Children under twelve must be accompanied by an adult. Phone: (503) 265-2863.

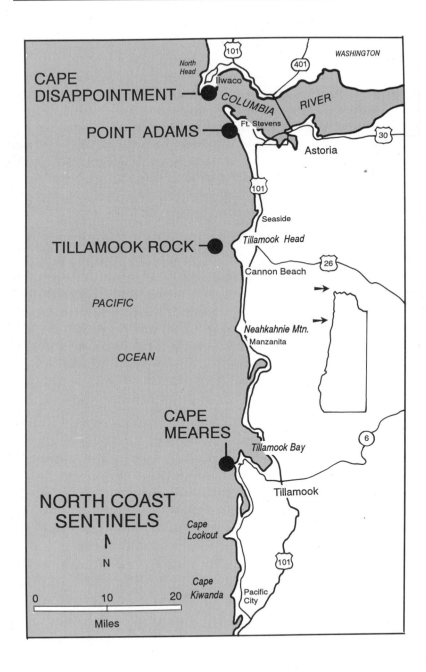

CAPE
DISAPPOINTMENT

North
Head

Ilwaco

COLUMBIA RIVER

WASHINGTON

101

401

POINT ADAMS

Ft. Stevens

Astoria

30

101

Seaside

TILLAMOOK ROCK

Tillamook Head

Cannon Beach

26

PACIFIC

Neahkahnie Mtn.

Manzanita

OCEAN

CAPE
MEARES

Tillamook Bay

6

NORTH COAST
SENTINELS

Tillamook

Cape
Lookout

N

Cape
Kiwanda

Pacific
City

101

0   10   20

Miles

52

Section 3

North Coast Sentinels

Though no explorers came to the Pacific Northwest between 1603 and 1774, ships still passed this way. They were Spanish galleons, laden with wealth from Manila on their way to Mexico. Their track was usually to the south, but at least one came upon Oregon's north coast. Tons of beeswax from the wreck of this galleon have been dug from the beach near the town of Manzanita, and legends persist of treasure buried on nearby Neahkahnie Mountain.

When the explorers returned, Spanish Captain Don Bruno de Heceta was among them. In 1775 he detected the Columbia River and might have discovered it for Spain, but his crew was too sick with scurvy to risk crossing the dangerous bar.

Thirteen years later, English trader John Meares looked for the river that Heceta had detected. After rounding a high cape, he encountered a wall of breakers extending to a low point in the south. Concluding that no river existed, he named the high cape "Disappointment."

In the same year American trader Robert Gray sailed his ship the *Lady Washington* into Tillamook Bay. His crew's logs provide the first written accounts of a ship entering an Oregon harbor.

The Northwest's first light shone from Cape Disappointment in 1856. Point Adams, the low point noted by Meares, received a light in 1875. Lights were later established at Cape Meares and on Tillamook Rock. The Cape Meares and Cape Disappointment lighthouse towers remain, and Tillamook's majestic tower can be seen from the shore.

TED NELSON

Visitors are greeted by this view of the Cape Meares Lighthouse after walking down a short trail.

Chapter 8

Cape Meares Lighthouse

The Cape Meares Lighthouse, a short, stout tower, is anchored to the outer edge of a high, bold headland just south of Tillamook Bay. The seaward face of Cape Meares is cut by near-vertical cliffs, and at the point where the tower stands, the cliffs drop nearly 200 feet to the waves below. Established in 1890, the tower is all that remains of the original lighthouse station.

Visitors to the lighthouse park their cars in the place once occupied by the keepers' dwelling, a barn, and gardens. From the parking lot, a long, straight path leads down through a corridor of trees to the lighthouse. Though the tower's base is hidden from view, the lantern room, framed by trees, looms large with its original first-order Fresnel lens inside. This is the same path the keepers used to tend the light. When gale winds blew, they had to crawl, for then there were no trees to buffer the wind.

Like the Yaquina Head Lighthouse, the Cape Meares Lighthouse has been plagued with the rumor that it was built in the wrong place. As the rumor goes, the tower should have been built on Cape Lookout, ten miles to the south. Records, however, show that the lighthouse was built at the location designated by the Lighthouse Board.

In January 1886 a bill was introduced in Congress to build a first-order light at Cape Meares. Before the bill was passed, the U.S. Army Corps of Engineers sent J. P. Polhemus to examine Cape Meares and Cape Lookout for a lighthouse site.

Polhemus spent several days in May on both capes, hiking old Indian

The Cape Meares Lighthouse with its first workroom. Circa 1900.

and bear trails. He camped out, taking measurements and compass bearings. To measure the height of Cape Meares, he dropped a marked cord down the cliff.

Polhemus reported that Cape Lookout "presents a very salient point for a Light House, and it more nearly divides the distance between the Light Houses on Tillamook Rk [sic] and at Cape Foulweather [Yaquina Head]. . . . " A lighthouse at Cape Lookout, however, would be higher than desirable, and it would be difficult to get building materials there.

"Cape Meares," Polhemus continued, " . . . affords nearly as good a site as far as the view from sea is concerned, and being lower gives a better situation of light with references to fog." Cape Meares also had a fresh water supply from a spring and easier access for delivering building materials.

In March 1887 Congress passed the bill to build a lighthouse on Cape Meares. A wagon road was built from the bay to the site, and construction began in the spring of 1889. Charles B. Duhrkoop, one of the contractors, built the tower's octagonal exterior walls with sheet iron made in Portland. The inside walls were lined with bricks made and fired on the site. By September the thirty-eight-foot-tall tower was completed.

A first-order Fresnel lens, made in France, was shipped to the cape in crates. It was assembled in the tower by matching the numbers inscribed on the brass frames of each section.

By late November, three men — Anthony Miller, principal keeper, and his two assistants, Andrew Hald and Henry York — had moved into the two new dwellings. On January 1, 1890, they wound the clockwork mechanism to rotate the lens, and they lit the five-wick kerosene lamp. The eight-paneled lens, including four with bullseyes and red screens, began to turn slowly. (Bullseyes are circular, convex lenses.) The lens exhibited a fixed white light, with a red flash every minute, that could be seen for twenty-one miles. There was no fog signal at the station.

Second assistant York was the only married man on the station. When he was settled, he sent for his wife and two children, ten-year-old Mabel and her three-year-old brother. The family left Portland for a three-day journey with a sewing machine, trunks, and crates packed with household goods. They traveled by steamer to Astoria, and the next day boarded a small schooner bound for Tillamook Bay.

York had alerted Indians living on the bay's shores to watch for them. When the family arrived, the Indians helped them come ashore and put them up for the night. The next morning the sewing machine, trunks, and crates were loaded on a flat sled and pulled up the steep, muddy road by four oxen. Mabel rode on one horse, her mother and brother on another.

Not all the outside work was completed when the family arrived. For several months they trudged about in mud and dirt until wooden walkways were built around the dwellings and down to the tower.

In a 1963 newspaper article, Mabel reminisced about her days at Cape Meares. She said she often accompanied her father to the tower and stayed with him during his watch. "I sat in a big chair reading a big book as we watched the clock [clockwork mechanism]." During the day, she watched him polish the lens' prisms, each one "shining like a diamond." One day while she was walking to the tower, gale winds flipped Mabel over. She grabbed a wood stake to keep from being blown over the cliff and clung to it until her father rescued her. Much as Mabel and her family enjoyed life at the lighthouse, they left after only one year. There were no schools nearby, and they moved so Mabel could continue her formal education.

Transportation was another problem. At that time the only route from the isolated station to Tillamook was down the muddy road on the north side of the cape, then up the bay by boat. Keepers timed their trips to town with the tides. At high tide, they could row the boat. At low tide, they had to pole the boat around mud flats.

This route, however, was an inadequate way to haul heavy materials from Tillamook for ongoing building projects. By 1894 a wagon road was built down the south side of the cape, then inland, where it connected with county roads. Now the keepers had a choice of routes: one timed by the tides or a seven-hour ride by buckboard.

In 1895 a badly needed brick workroom was built at the base of the tower. Workrooms added comfort to a keeper's watch, especially on cold winter nights. There was a desk, a chair, and a wood stove which kept the keepers warm and the tower's interior dry.

During the next decade, life at the lighthouse station mirrored life in town, complete with a wedding, births, schooling, and a funeral.

George Hunt and his wife and children moved to Cape Meares when he was assigned principal keeper in January 1892. Several men assisted

Cape Meares, now covered with trees, was once a stark setting for the lighthouse and the storage houses for the lamp's fuel.

Hunt during the 1890s before George H. Higgins was appointed second assistant keeper in January 1901.

Higgins, a dapper young bachelor, wore a mustache and his dark hair parted in the middle. During his first year at the station, he courted Amelia M. Freeman, the daughter of a Tillamook pioneer family. On Christmas Day 1901, the couple was married at the lighthouse station. A photo displayed in the tower shows Amelia wearing a white wedding gown and George in his Lighthouse Service uniform with a white shirt and tie.

In the spring of 1903 Higgins, then a proud new father, was promoted to first assistant keeper. Two months later keeper Hunt became ill. On July 7, 1903, the lighthouse log entry read, "Attended to regular duties. Keeper sick with pneumonia." The entry was repeated each day until July 10, when a new entry read, "Commenced haying. Keeper died at 6 p.m." Hunt's funeral was held in Tillamook two days later. His widow served as acting principal keeper until August 2: "Keeper wife, Mrs. and children left station today."

The new principal keeper, Harry Mahler, arrived with his wife and three children a few days later. Mahler, mid-way in his forty-two-year career in the Lighthouse Service, had been transferred from Patos Island Lighthouse in Washington's San Juan Islands.

When the Mahlers arrived, there was a one-room schoolhouse about a mile away. The Mahler children and the assistant keeper's two daughters attended school during the summer months. With lunch buckets in hand, the five children rode two horses to school.

When Mahler left in 1907, Higgins was promoted to principal keeper, and then resigned two years later. He, his wife, and three daughters — all born at the lighthouse station — moved to Portland where Higgins entered the real estate business.

Only minor changes came to the station during the following years. In 1910 the original heavy bronze lamp was replaced by an oil vapor lamp. This eliminated the daily chore of trimming the wicks, but not the chore of winding the clockwork machinery. About every four hours the keeper on watch had to crank up the heavy weights by hand. If the mechanism failed, the keeper turned the lens by hand until morning, when repairs could be made.

The keepers' work was made easier in 1934 when two generators were installed to provide electricity to the tower. An electric light replaced the oil vapor lamp, and an electric motor rotated the lens. The two small buildings where oil for the lamp had been stored were torn down.

Cape Meares was one of the first Oregon lighthouses automated on the coast. A small concrete building holding a modern optic was built on the ledge above the tower. Then the original lens was decommissioned on April 1, 1963, and the new optic, flashing white, was switched on to operate twenty-four hours a day unattended.

The two Coast Guard keepers and their families moved away and the workroom was razed. When the Coast Guard was ready to raze the tower, local citizens rallied. They succeeded in saving the lens and tower and having the property leased to Tillamook County in 1964.

Four years later the county turned its lease over to Oregon State Parks, and the station was opened to the public. During this time, the dwellings were vandalized, and the four bullseyes were stolen from the lens. The dwellings, too damaged to save, were torn down, and a parking lot was laid over the spot. A replica of the old workroom was built, but its door is on the south side for better visitor access. On Memorial Day 1980, the lighthouse was opened for visitors. The lens, however, was still missing its bullseyes.

Then, one by one, three were recovered. The first was found in Portland during a drug raid in 1984. Two years later an article in a regional magazine requested the return of the other three bullseyes, no questions asked. Within days after the article appeared, one was left at the Tillamook County Pioneer Museum.

A week later, Michael Hewitt, assistant park manager, and his family arrived at their Cape Lookout State Park home in the pouring rain. While his wife Theresea and their two sons waited in the car, Hewitt ran to unlock the front door. Wedged behind the screen door was a burlap bag. Hewitt opened it and grinned. It was the third lens. "He held it up like a kid with a piece of candy," Theresea recalled. The bullseyes will be restored and eventually remounted in the lens.

Today a gift shop and interpretive displays are located in the workroom and the lower floor of the tower. Visitors can climb the iron steps inside the tower to the lantern room, where the original first-order Fresnel lens is displayed.

The modern optic still serves mariners, but lacks the warm glow of the original light, which shone on Mabel York, sitting in the tower at night and reading her big book.

Directions and Hours: Cape Meares is nine miles west of Tillamook. Follow signs for Netarts, Oceanside, and Cape Lookout State Park, then signs to Cape Meares State Park. The park is open year-round. The lighthouse is open daily, June through September from 11 A.M. to 5 P.M. Phone Cape Lookout State Park (the headquarters for Cape Meares) at (503) 842-4981.

Also, visit the Tillamook Pioneer Museum, 2106 Second Street in Tillamook. Phone: (503) 842-4553.

A boat from a lighthouse tender cautiously approaches the Tillamook Rock Lighthouse in high winds.

Chapter 9

Tillamook Rock Lighthouse

The Tillamook Rock Lighthouse stands on a wave-washed basaltic knob that protrudes from the sea about a mile off Tillamook Head. In its description of the rock, the 1889 *Coast Pilot* stated that a "great swell of the Pacific from [the] southwest rolls with tremendous force upon this rocky islet . . . waters are driven in with great fury. . . . "

William Hill, who retired as the lighthouse's principal keeper in 1936, called it "the most thrilling station on the Pacific Coast, principally because of the terrific storms and seas that batter it." Descriptions such as these led the lighthouse to be nicknamed "Terrible Tilly."

In the 1800s, Tillamook Head was an important landfall for mariners approaching the Columbia River, twenty miles to the north, and in 1878 Congress authorized funds for a lighthouse on the head. Major George Gillespie, the Lighthouse Service engineer, however, concluded that a lighthouse there often would be obscured by fog, and would require building twenty miles of road.

Instead, he recommended that the lighthouse and fog signal be built on Tillamook Rock, despite its being a "task of labor and difficulty, accompanied by great expense." The Lighthouse Board agreed.

Except for Maine's Minots Ledge Lighthouse, no other lighthouse had yet offered construction challenges like those of Tillamook Rock. Seas were seldom calm, and the rock's steep, jagged sides made it hazardous to jump from a surfboat onto the rock. In September 1879, a surveyor slipped and drowned while trying to reach the rock.

A few days after the accident, Charles A. Ballantyne was appointed

OREGON HISTORICAL SOCIETY-55389

The Tillamook Rock Lighthouse on a calm day. In storms, waves carrying rocks broke over the tower.

superintendent. He quickly hired eight quarrymen, but the Revenue Service vessel *Corwin*, assigned to take the men to the rock, could not cross the Columbia's bar due to bad weather. Gillespie told Ballantyne to keep the men "free from the idle talk of the town [about the surveyor's death]," so the crew was sequestered in the original keepers' dwelling at Cape Disappointment until conditions on the bar improved.

On October 21, two men leaped to the rock's slippery surface. They stretched a 300-foot cable from the top of the rock to the *Corwin*. A traveler hooked to the cable delivered hammers, drills, iron ring-bolts, a stove, and canvas for temporary shelter. The men rode back and forth sitting in a breeches buoy, a seat made from a life ring fitted with old pants cut off at the knees. The breeches buoy, though safer than leaping from a boat, was no drier. As the *Corwin* rolled, the cable slacked, and the passenger was dunked in the cold sea. After a few months, a derrick was built which could lift supplies and personnel to the rock from a boat below.

Once safely on the rock, the men bolted a timber shanty to the surface for living quarters, built a supply shed, and began leveling the bulging top of the rock. Hanging on ropes, often swinging out over the sea, they carefully placed cartridges and black powder in the rock's fissures, lit the fuses, then scurried to take cover before the explosion.

Slowly, tons of basalt were blasted away and pushed into the sea. The men worked through fog, rain, and wind, stopping only when seas breached the rock. In seven months the crew blasted away nearly 4,600 cubic yards of basalt, reducing the knob's height by thirty feet to create a pad for the lighthouse.

On June 22, 1880, the lighthouse cornerstone was laid, and construction began. Stone was quarried near Portland and cut to size before delivery. The first layer of stone was bolted into the rock. The layers of stone above were held tightly in place by iron straps.

Even while the men worked, the need for a light and fog signal on Tillamook Rock became apparent. Ballentyne twice heard the whistle of an approaching steamer. He tossed cartridges of exploding powder over the water, and the sound of the blast warned the ships to veer away.

One evening, only days before the light was lit, a storm lashed the rock. From the darkness, the workers heard shouts and the creaking of a ship's blocks. It was the English iron bark *Laputa*. Quickly, the men lit lanterns and threw kerosene on driftwood to light a signal fire. Sounds from the ship faded in the howling wind. The next morning the men saw the ship wrecked on the mainland. All sixteen people on board had drowned.

The lighthouse's flashing white light was exhibited for the first time on January 21, 1881, from a first-order Fresnel lens, 133 feet above the water. The sixty-two-foot-high square tower protruded from the center of the one-story stone dwelling. There was a room for each keeper, a kitchen, and a storeroom to hold supplies for six months. The fog signal, a siren, was housed in an annex adjoining the dwelling, and a cistern, carved deep into the rock, collected rain for the station's water supply.

Five men were assigned to the lighthouse, four working while the fifth was on shore leave. Because of the isolation and difficulties involved in tending the station, no families or female keepers lived on Tillamook Rock.

Within three weeks, the new keepers experienced their first heavy storm. A keeper wrote that the "Building [was] badly flooded inside and out. There might as well be no windows." The lighthouse's sashes and iron shutters fit badly, so while two men took their turns standing watch in the tower, the others tried to plug the holes.

Despite the new station's isolation, the keepers had their share of visitors. Before the lighthouse was built, the rock had been home to hundreds of sea lions, and some of them returned after the workmen left. One keeper found a sea lion asleep on the doorstep. "Rather startling to open the door on a dark night to be confronted with such a visitor," he wrote.

Formal visitors arrived on June 22, 1881, the first anniversary of the laying of the cornerstone. For the occasion, Major Gillespie and others from Portland and Astoria arrived by boat and were lifted onto the rock in a basket suspended from the end of the derrick.

Although the anniversary visitors arrived on schedule, weather conditions often caused the keepers to wait for weeks before vessels could bring them mail and supplies. In May 1882 the keepers had only beans and flour left to eat. They repaired the station boat, damaged in a storm, and tried fishing. "Not even a bite," wrote the keeper. "No meat, no coffee, no sugar, no pickles, and no fish, in fact we have nothing but dissatisfaction at the way we are treated." That evening the tender *Shubrick* steamed alongside, but the seas were too rough for it to land provisions, so the ship turned back, only adding to the keepers' frustration.

Life at the station was not always glum. There were calm days when the keepers cleaned flower pots and planted radish and lettuce seed. Swallows nested at the station, and one keeper noted in the log book that "the young swallow had her first fly today." In July 1893 the keeper wrote that "Six ladies visited the rock and spent a happy time here."

Still, the winter storms came, bringing walls of water over the lighthouse. Rocks carried by the waves knocked holes in the dwelling's roof and broke the lantern's glass. Fearful of being blown or washed away, the men dared not venture outside. Yet, while struggling to make repairs, the keepers managed to keep the light shining.

Keeper Hill was at Tillamook Rock during a storm that lasted four days. On October 21, 1934, the Oregon and Washington coasts were hit with winds up to 100 miles per hour. The gale-lashed waves tore at the rock and threw 100-pound fragments at the tower. The lantern's glass was broken. To replace the broken glass with storm shutters, the keepers worked in water up to their necks in the lantern room. Then the water broke through a door and poured down the tower's throat, flooding the quarters below and depositing barnacles, small fish, and seaweed. The derrick was washed away, and the lens was severely damaged. But the keepers rigged an auxiliary light, so the tower was dark for only one night.

Using scraps and parts from a useless telephone, its underwater cable torn out in the storm, first assistant keeper Henry Jenkins built a short-wave radio. On October 23, he reached an amateur radio operator on the mainland, who informed lighthouse officials of conditions on the rock. News of the keepers' heroics reached the national press, and each received a commendation from the Superintendent of Lighthouses.

The repair work done that winter proved to be as difficult as building the lighthouse. Another breeches buoy had to be rigged until a new derrick could be built. Repairs were completed by February 1935, and in June a new lens was set in place to replace the original, damaged lens.

Some keepers didn't mind the storms and loneliness on the rock. William Dahlgren served for twenty years at the lighthouse, beginning in 1901, even though he had a family living ashore. One year bad weather forced Dahlgren to stay on the rock for eleven months. On Thanksgiving the tender couldn't land any provisions, including the one thing all the keepers desired — a turkey. Fate (and the wind) supplied their dinner: two ducks crashed into the lantern and fell dead on the metal gallery. Hours later the keepers feasted on roast duck.

Oswald Allik also served for twenty years, beginning in 1937. He was a civilian first assistant keeper when coast guardsman James Gibbs arrived to help tend the station in 1945. In his book, *Tillamook Light*, Gibbs relates his year at the station. Though less than happy with his new assignment — standing watch and listening to the "powerful roar" of the fog signal — Gibbs fulfilled his duties. On leaving, he wrote that he was "going to miss the natural surroundings; the untamed, changing seascape and the moods of weather."

Allik was the last principal keeper at Tillamook Rock. By 1957 the lighthouse had become the most expensive in the nation to operate. The Coast Guard closed the station and replaced it with an ocean buoy about

Two keepers relax in the kitchen of the Tillamook Rock Lighthouse.

one mile distant.

In his final log entry, Allik wrote, "Farewell Tillamook Rock Light Station, an era has ended without sentiment. I return thee to the elements. . . . " At one minute past midnight on September 10, 1957, he switched off the light.

Within two years after closing, the station was sold. The purchasers, a Nevada business group, paid $5,600 for the station, but never used it. It was sold two more times, each time at a higher price. In 1980 it was sold again to Portland realtors for $50,000.

The realtors came up with the idea of creating a cemetery at sea. The lighthouse was entered on the National Register of Historic Sites, the building was refurbished, and the windows and lantern were walled in. The interior was designed to hold nearly a half million urns containing human ashes. To celebrate completion of the Eternity at Sea Columbarium, a centennial party for the laying of the cornerstone was held on Tillamook Rock in June 1980, with guests arriving by helicopter.

As a private facility, the Tillamook Rock Lighthouse is not open to the public. It can be seen from Ecola State Park, Cannon Beach, and Seaside.

68

Chapter 10

Point Adams Lighthouse

For twenty-four years, the Point Adams Lighthouse stood proudly on an ocean beach south of the mouth of the Columbia River. Established in 1875, it was unique among Oregon lighthouses. It was the first Oregon light station with a steam fog signal and was the only one built in the Victorian Carpenters' Gothic style.

Today the station is gone, and the landscape has changed. At one time Point Adams was a rounded point at the river's entrance, a half mile from the ocean. The 1869 *Coast Pilot* described it as "low and sandy, covered with bushes and trees to the line of sand beach and low dunes. . . . " Now an enlarged Clatsop Spit separates the point from the sea by nearly one and one half miles. The spit expanded to the west and northwest after jetty construction, begun in the 1880s, altered currents around the point.

The Columbia's entrance, where the river clashes with the sea, is one of the roughest, most treacherous stretches of water in the United States, and has claimed hundreds of ships. One of the first navigation aids built to assist mariners crossing the river's bar was the Cape Disappointment Lighthouse, established on the north side of the river in 1856. With the passing years, more ships used the channel on the south side, and Lighthouse Service engineers urged the building of a light and fog signal at Point Adams.

In 1873 a site about a mile from the point was selected for the new station. It was near the southwest boundary of Fort Stevens, a river fortification established in the mid-1860s.

An unknown resident occupied the Point Adams Lighthouse after it was discontinued in 1899.

Shortly after a public announcement appeared regarding the site selection, district engineer Major Henry Robert received a letter of protest signed by "The Masters of Steam Ships, Sailing Ships and Pilots." They expressed doubts about the suitability of a light and fog signal at Point Adams. They recommended the station be built on Sand Island, north and upstream of the river's entrance. Their reasons: ocean breakers would render a Point Adams fog signal inaudible to vessels approaching from the south; better bearings could be taken with a station on Sand Island when entering the river; and in low fog a captain guided by a fog signal there could shape his course by following the depth of the channel.

Major Robert replied by assuring the masters that Point Adams would have a "fog signal of the very greatest power," and a light there "will be low and will often be seen when Cape Hancock (Cape Disappointment) is obscured by fog." He added that a light on Sand Island "would help and may in time be justified."

Materials were landed at the Fort Stevens wharf on the Columbia River and hauled south over a road to the site. At the time Victorian architecture was in vogue, and the Lighthouse Service decided to use a Carpenters' Gothic design for the wooden Point Adams Lighthouse. Jigsaws had just been invented and were used to cut wood into ornate patterns for the building's interior and exterior trim.

The Lighthouse Service built five Carpenters' Gothic lighthouses during the 1870s, four in California and the one at Point Adams. Two remain: the East Brother Island Lighthouse near San Francisco and the Point Fermin Lighthouse in San Pedro. The latter is almost an exact copy of the one that stood on Point Adams.

A light was first exhibited from a fourth-order Fresnel lens in the Point Adams tower on February 15, 1875. The combination dwelling and tower stood on a sand ridge with the forest behind and ocean beaches in front.

The fog signal was as Major Robert had promised. Its twelve-inch, locomotive-type whistle, powered by steam, was one of the most powerful fog signals then available.

With a signal and light to operate, three keepers were assigned to Point Adams. H. C. Tracy was the first principal keeper. In 1878 he was replaced by Robert N. Lowe, an Astoria boat builder. Lowe moved in with his new wife, and before long their son Edward was born at the lighthouse.

Joel Munson replaced Lowe as principal keeper in late 1880. Munson was a skilled violinist and often played for dances in Astoria and for lighthouse visitors. Clara, his daughter, once wrote, "Both young and old, felt at liberty to enjoy the hospitality afforded by the out hanging latch-string, and it was no uncommon thing for 2 or 3 wagon loads of friends to drive from Fort Stevens, Hammond or Skipanon in the evening. Then the old violin would be brought out and the hours would fly by."

While keepers at other stations cultivated dark soil to grow gardens, Munson and his Point Adams predecessors fought the drifting sand. It blew into the dwelling, completely covered the picket fence, and threatened the station's water supply. Long, tall fences were built and rebuilt to try to control the sand. Grass plantings were tried with little success except one, a native grass. However, when the bright green shoots appeared above the sand, cattle ate them. Then barbed wire fences were built to keep the cattle out.

During Munson's service at the Cape Disappointment Lighthouse, he had saved passengers and crews from two sinking ships. Now, at Point Adams, Munson participated in significant changes and witnessed more shipwrecks. On January 21, 1881, the same day the light at Tillamook Rock was lit, Point Adams' light characteristic was changed from flashing red to fixed red. Later that year these two changes caused an accident. According to Don Marshall in *Oregon Shipwrecks*, the captain of the British ship *Fern Glen* was unaware of the new Tillamook Rock light and Point Adams' new characteristic. He became confused and his ship ploughed into Clatsop Spit.

One smokey September afternoon in 1883, the *Cairnsmore* grounded on the beach. The crew, not sure where they were, jumped in the lifeboats and headed out to sea. They were picked up by a passing vessel and taken to Astoria. Had they remained on board and waited for the outgoing tide, they could have walked ashore. The ship was never salvaged. For years it lay buried in the sand with only its masts visible.

Just as the ships' masters predicted, the noise of the surf in front of the lighthouse made the fog signal inaudible to passing vessels. It was discontinued after five years of service. The boiler and signal apparatus were removed, stored at the Tongue Point Depot, then shipped to Washington's Point Robinson on Puget Sound. Here it began operating once again in 1885.

Without a fog signal to tend, the remaining assistant left. (The first had left about a year earlier when his position was eliminated.) The Munson family then lived alone in the big dwelling, and Munson's daughter, Clara, helped him tend the light.

Four years after the fog signal was discontinued, an unofficial signal began helping vessels cross the south side of the Columbia's mouth. When work on the south river jetty began, hoisting engines with steam whistles were installed at the Fort Stevens wharf to lift rock from barges onto rail cars. While the hoisting engines were in place, it became the practice to blow their steam whistles "during fogs in response to any steamer sounding its whistle and trying to find its way along the channels and this has been a great assistance to navigation," reported the district inspector.

The Lighthouse Board decided that when the hoisting engines and their whistles were gone, a fog signal and harbor light should be built to take their place. They would discontinue Point Adams, use some of its equipment, and establish a new lighthouse station near the wharf at Fort Stevens.

Only one suitable site could be found, but it was tied up in a lawsuit between private parties and the War Department. Other sites were reserved for Fort Stevens' gun batteries. The Lighthouse Board then recommended and eventually received funding to build a new station on Desdemona Sands.

Munson, the last keeper to tend the Point Adams Lighthouse, left in October 1898, and the station was officially discontinued on January 31, 1899. Thirteen years later the Lighthouse Service burned down the abandoned station.

Before the lighthouse's destruction, a steel bark named the *Peter Iredale* was blown ashore nearby. All on board were saved, though this time keeper Joel Munson was not there to assist in the rescue. The ship's rusting bones still protrude above the sand and are a tourist attraction today.

Directions and Hours: Today the Point Adams Lighthouse is gone. Fort Stevens' Battery Russell, built in 1904, stands near the site where the lighthouse once stood. To visit the site, follow signs in Hammond for Fort Stevens State Park and Battery Russell. The park is open year-round. Phone: (503) 861-1671.

SHARLENE NELSON

The Cape Disappointment Lighthouse is still operating and is the oldest in the Pacific Northwest.

Chapter 11

Cape Disappointment Lighthouse

The light from the Cape Disappointment tower was the first to shine across Pacific Northwest waters. Lit on October 15, 1856, it is still shining today. Although located in Washington on the north side of the Columbia River's entrance, this lighthouse was built to guide mariners safely along Oregon's north coast and into the Columbia on their way to ports upriver.

Cape Disappointment, a prominent tree-covered headland rising nearly 300 feet above the water, was named by English fur trader John Meares. In 1788 Meares sailed beneath the cape looking for the river that Spanish explorers had claimed was there. Deciding that no such river existed, he sailed away, leaving behind the name "Cape Disappointment."

After the discovery of the Columbia by Captain Robert Gray, the river became the busiest waterway in the Pacific Northwest, spurred first by the fur trade and later by settlement. Cape Disappointment became an important landfall. Early mariners guided by the cape as they sailed the coast and crossed the treacherous waters at the river's entrance, where, one mariner wrote, "Mere description can give little idea of the terrors of the bar . . . the wildness of scene and the incessant roar of the waters."

Unofficial beacons first appeared on the cape in 1812. Men from Fort Astor (now Astoria), wanting to assist the arrival of their supply ship, flew a white flag from a tree. They also set fire to the trees at night to serve, as they said, "in lieu of a lighthouse." Years later, three trees on the cape were cut off at the top. From five miles offshore, mariners took bearings on the trimmed trees and steered for the deepest channel beneath the cape.

The cape therefore became the logical place to locate the first lighthouse in the Pacific Northwest. In 1848, when lawmakers drew up the act to create Oregon Territory (which included present-day Oregon and Washington), they made a provision for a lighthouse at Cape Disappointment.

Five years later, the Baltimore, Maryland, firm of Gibbons and Kelley began to build the first lighthouses on the Pacific Coast, including the one on Cape Disappointment. After work was near completion on four California lighthouses in 1853, the company's ship *Oriole*, carrying building materials and workmen, arrived at the Columbia in September. As it crossed the bar, the winds dropped, leaving the ship at the mercy of the currents and waves. The *Oriole* sank and its cargo was lost, but its crew and the workmen survived.

A year later a second ship arrived with materials. Soon a fifty-three-foot, white-washed tower built of brick and stone stood on the cape, 220 feet above the river. Then another delay occurred. A new lighting system, using Fresnel lenses, was ordered after the tower was designed. As a result, the tower was too small to hold the first-order lens and had to be rebuilt.

At last a fixed white light shone from the tower. Nearby, a 1,600-pound fog bell hung outside a small wood-frame building that housed the striking mechanism.

In the late 1850s, seventeen-year-old George Easterbrook was assigned as second assistant at the lighthouse. His remembrances later appeared in Pacific County's Historical Quarterly, *The So'Wester.*

Easterbrook shared the dwelling, about a quarter-mile from the tower, on the east side of the cape, with the principal keeper, his family, and one other assistant. They had no neighbors. The closest town was Astoria, fifteen miles southeast across the Columbia River. Paid quarterly, the keepers sailed in their small boat to Astoria to draw their earnings from the customs officer.

During each watch, Easterbrook worked diligently to keep the lamp lit. The lamp, with five concentric wicks and a first-order lens, Easterbrook said, created "a solid mass of light almost rivaling the sun. . . . "

The lamp consumed over five gallons of whale oil each night. One stormy night when, in Easterbrook's words, "the swaying and rocking motion of the tower at this height was something to brace against . . . " the oil pumps slowed, starving the wicks. The light nearly flickered out.

Holiday visitors at the Cape Disappointment Lighthouse. Circa 1890.

Fearing the customs officer would see the dimmed light and withhold his pay, Easterbrook hurriedly restarted the pumps.

A well-known principal keeper at Cape Disappointment during its first decades was Captain Joel Munson. Munson, who had lived near Astoria, was assigned to the station in 1865, and while there started a lifesaving station.

Munson had been on duty only a few months when he watched helplessly as the bark *Industry* sank nearby. For two weeks the ship had stood off the entrance, waiting to enter the river. The captain, tired of battling the stormy weather, decided to cross the bar. The ship went aground in the north channel. Seventeen people drowned; only seven survived.

According to Emma Gene Miller in her book, *Clatsop County, Oregon,* when wreckage from the Industry washed ashore, "Munson found an old metallic boat containing air tanks . . . so he conceived the idea that this boat could be put to good order and used for rescue work." Munson raised money for the boat's repair by holding dances in Astoria and charging $2.50 per person. To help Munson, the Lighthouse Service built a boathouse for the boat.

Munson's rescuing skills would be needed the following year. He and a volunteer crew pushed off in the repaired lifeboat to save the passengers and crew aboard the sinking ship *W. B. Scranton*. All thirteen people were rescued.

Munson had demonstrated the success of a rescue service at the cape. In 1878 a U.S. Life-Saving Service Station was established at Cape Disappointment. Munson left the Lighthouse Service and returned to Astoria and shipbuilding. Lightkeeping, however, had not lost its appeal, and he became principal keeper at Point Adams Lighthouse in 1881.

Because of the cape's strategic location at the mouth of the Columbia, it was selected as a site for one of three forts to guard the river's entrance during the Civil War. Initially, four cannon were mounted at Lighthouse Battery, next to the lighthouse. In 1871 practice firing shattered the fog bell house, and a new one was built.

For twenty-five years, the keepers faithfully tended the fog bell, forced to listen to its incessant bonging: nine consecutive blows each minute, hour after hour. Still, the bell was not always heard by vessels approaching the bar. On September 1, 1881, the bell was discontinued and sent north to Washington's new West Point Lighthouse. Later, it clanged its warning at the Warrior Rock Lighthouse.

For many years one lighthouse seemed sufficient to mark this headland. But mariners approaching from the north couldn't see the Cape Disappointment light, which caused several shipwrecks on beaches north of the cape.

In 1889 the Lighthouse Board began plans to build a coastal tower for a first-order lens on the cape's North Head, about two miles from the Cape Disappointment Lighthouse. When the North Head Lighthouse was built in 1898, Cape Disappointment's first-order lens was moved to North Head. A new fourth-order Fresnel lens with red screens was installed in its place. This lens is still operating. The first-order lens was later removed from North Head and is now on display at the Lewis and Clark Interpretive Center at Fort Canby State Park.

Not until World War II was the Cape Disappointment tower ever dark at night. A few days after war was declared, navigation lights at the Columbia River's entrance were extinguished temporarily to observe a Pacific Coast blackout. On December 10, 1941, a distress signal was received from the steamship *Mauna Ala*. The ship, bound for Honolulu with a cargo of Christmas trees and decorations, was ordered to return to Seattle. The captain was unaware of the blackout and ran the ship aground on Clatsop Spit just south of the Columbia River. The captain and crew were saved, but the cargo and ship were lost.

In 1965 the Cape Disappointment tower came close to being permanently darkened. The Coast Guard felt that the river's entrance was adequately marked by lighted buoys and the Columbia River Lightship, and planned to discontinue the faithful old lighthouse. When bar pilots protested, however, the plans were withdrawn.

The lighthouse was automated in 1973, and is now monitored by a computer in the Aids to Navigation Team office in Astoria. Though the tower is closed, visitors can walk around the outside. Perhaps someday they'll be able to go inside as well. In 1994, discussions were being held about turning the lighthouse over to Washington State Parks. Many visitors then would have the opportunity to climb the stairs in the oldest operating structure in Washington.

Directions and Hours: From downtown Ilwaco, follow signs to Cape Disappointment and Fort Canby State Park. Park in the Lewis and Clark Interpretive Center lot and follow the signed trail to the lighthouse. The interpretive center is open daily from May through September from 9 A.M. to 5 P.M. From October through April the center is open, but each season the hours change. Call the park for information: (206) 642-3029.

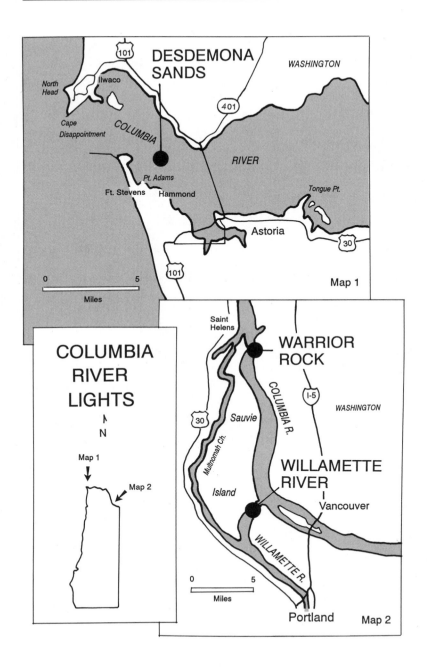

Section 4

Columbia River Lights

In 1792 American Captain Robert Gray sailed into the "Great River of the West," which he named after his ship, the *Columbia Redeviva*. Seeking sea otter pelts from Chinook Indians for trade with China, he found the river that had eluded explorers for nearly 200 years.

Not long after Gray's discovery, the sea otter trade gave way to the beaver fur trade. With it came the dominance of England's Hudson's Bay Company over the Pacific Northwest. Chief Factor John McLoughlin, the man in charge of the company's operations in the region, befriended Americans coming west on the Oregon Trail beginning in the 1840s. The presence of these settlers, along with Gray's discovery of the Columbia, led to the establishment of Oregon Territory in 1848.

Early settlers began building towns, farms, sawmills, and gristmills along the lower Columbia and the Willamette River. Their small enterprises flourished with the discovery of gold in California. In 1850, 160 ships sailed down the Columbia with lumber, flour, and produce, bound mostly for California.

Today, ocean-going vessels steam pass riverside roadways to reach ports as far inland as Portland. Their presence belies the dangers that early mariners faced on the river. Before being tamed by jetties, dams, and dredging, the river was a maze of shoals and sloughs.

To combat these hazards, three lighthouse stations were established along the river: Desdemona Sands, Warrior Rock, and Willamette River. Only a small tower at Warrior Rock remains.

The Desdemona Sands light and fog signal station was perched on piles in the Columbia River.

Chapter 12

Desdemona Sands Lighthouse

Now no longer standing, the Desdemona Sands Lighthouse had been operating for only eight days on January 1, 1903. The assistant keeper noted in his log that several of the ships anchored near the light station welcomed the New Year with "ringing bells, singing, music, and general good cheer."

New Year's Day forty-six years earlier had witnessed a different scene. Near the place where the lighthouse would later be built, the bark *Desdemona* lay stranded in the sand. According to historian Lancaster Pollard, the ship's captain had been offered a new suit of Sunday clothes if he entered the Columbia River by January 1, thus saving the owners a late delivery penalty. The vessel grounded when the captain, unable to secure a pilot, rushed his ship into the river unassisted. Some of the cargo was salvaged, but the ship could not be recovered. It gave its name to the sands where it lay.

The Desdemona Sands are a large area of shoals inside the river's mouth and north of the main channel. The lighthouse, built to replace the abandoned Point Adams station, stood on piles at the shoals' west end, about four miles from Astoria.

The lamp was lit for the first time on Christmas Eve 1902. According to the log, the days before the lighting were busy. The tender *Manzanita* delivered coal, cases of mineral oil, soap, and one library book. Carpenters came to put finishing touches on the station's woodwork, and engineers arrived to fine-tune the fog signal's machinery.

The day before the lighting, a storm blew in and rain leaked into the building. When the lighting took place on Christmas Eve, according to the log, "the lamp burned fine . . . considering the high wind and the sway of the building."

The lighthouse, a wood-frame two-and-one-half-story building, stood on a platform above a maze of piles. A lantern at the roof's center held a fourth-order Fresnel lens. The flaring tube of the fog signal, a Daboll trumpet, protruded towards the river's bar from the building's west end. The east end of the platform held an oil room and two 3,000-gallon cisterns. Tenders could tie up to a small wharf at the station's south side.

The first principal keeper assigned to the lighthouse, Thomas Gibson, missed the commissioning. Before he reached the station, he was reassigned to the Tillamook Rock light. His replacement, Frank Wyman, arrived aboard the *Manzanita* on January 16 along with more coal and firewood.

Alex Karlson replaced Wyman as principal keeper in 1908. Karlson was one of many early keepers who began their careers at sea. A Finlander, he boarded his first vessel at the age of twelve, and by age twenty-one had sailed around Cape Horn numerous times. He then served on lighthouse tenders, and at the age of thirty-seven became assistant keeper at Desdemona Sands in 1905. After a brief tour at Washington's Destruction Island Lighthouse, he returned to Desdemona Sands to serve as principal keeper from 1907 to 1914. Then he tended the inner harbor lights at Grays Harbor, Washington, for twenty years.

Unlike most other lighthouse stations, the Desdemona Sands Lighthouse never became a home for the principal keeper, his assistant, and their families. Helga Settles remembers this as she describes her husband's assignment there. Arvel Settles had served at California's Point Arguello and Point Arena lighthouses before coming to Desdemona Sands as assistant keeper in the mid-1920s.

Helga, now a resident of Friday Harbor, Washington, said, "It was not my favorite lighthouse, because I had to live in Hammond with our four children while Arvel and the principal keeper alternated tending the lighthouse." Sometimes Arvel would be gone for weeks at a time. During these periods, Helga regularly took the children out in a small rowboat with an outboard engine to visit their father at the lighthouse.

While Settles was at the station, a reed horn fog signal was operating in place of the original Daboll trumpet. In 1934, a submerged power cable was laid to a small tower near the station, and a new electrically operated fog signal was installed. The fog signal and a new electric beacon could be activated from shore. Keepers were no longer needed at the station, or so it seemed on October 23, 1934, when the keeper wrote, "To Day is Finis at station. Left at 4 P.M."

Two days later, however, the log entries resumed with, "Ordered to return to station . . . new [fog] signal out of commission. . . . " The keeper spent the next few days operating the old fog signal and overseeing unsuccessful efforts to repair the new one. He made numerous crossings in the station's small boat through the wind and fog to pick up supplies and assistance in the nearby town of Hammond.

On November 2 the tender *Rose* arrived at the station with mechanics and a wrecking crew. The mechanics repaired and started the fog signal, and the wrecking crew began to dismantle the roof-top lantern. A squall struck as the lantern was being removed. Rain poured through the opening, flooding the quarters below. The keeper, now sleeping in his raincoat and rubber boots, awoke to find that the new signal had failed again.

The mechanics returned and took part of the signal to the Tongue Point Depot for repairs. A tarp, stretched over the lantern's opening, was partially blown away in another storm. As water sloshed in every room, the fog signal was finally repaired. The keeper and his assistant readied the station for evacuation.

On November 6 the *Rose* arrived to take away almost everything that could be moved. The tender departed, and the keeper's log recorded, this time with finality, "This is finish of this station for sure."

In 1965, the fog signal and beacon were replaced by a series of lighted buoys. Only a few broken piles and riprap stones now mark the place where the lighthouse stood and where the *Desdemona* once lay.

Warrior Rock's bell can be seen in the small wooden tower. Circa 1890.

Chapter 13

Warrior Rock Lighthouse

A small white tower, its light showing twenty-eight feet above the water, is all that remains of this 1889 station. Though never imposing, this station near Warrior Point, on the northern tip of Sauvie Island, marked an area critical to river navigators.

The cement tower stands on a rock that juts into the Columbia River. The rock constricts the channel opposite the Lewis River's confluence and presents a hazard to passing vessels. Downriver, the Multnomah Channel meets the Columbia. The rock's constriction, combined with sediments from the Lewis River and the Multnomah Channel, created hazardous shoals near the busy shipbuilding and lumber town of Saint Helens. Early river sailors knew this area as the Saint Helens bar.

Warrior Point and Warrior Rock earned their names at the time of the arrival of Lieutenant W. R. Broughton in 1792. Broughton was a member of Captain George Vancouver's voyage of discovery, and he was the first European to explore the Columbia beyond its lower estuary. When his small boat approached the point, it was surrounded by twenty-three canoes carrying Indians dressed for battle. Though no fighting occurred, the name "Warrior," given by Broughton, became attached to the point and the rock.

In 1877 the Lighthouse Service established the first lights on the river at the Saint Helens bar to mark a channel recently dredged by the U.S. Army Corps of Engineers. The lights were two small red lanterns, mounted on tripods and cared for by contracted keepers.

As lighting of the lower Columbia continued, the Lighthouse Service endeavored to buy the property at Warrior Rock for a fog signal station in 1877. The owner refused to sell, and in 1888, 39/100 of an acre was acquired by condemnation. A construction contract was approved in June 1889.

All that was needed was a stone and masonry pier with a wooden tower on top to house the fog bell, its striking mechanism, and a small lens lantern. There were no funds or room to build a dwelling. Keepers lived in a rented bungalow until 1913, when it was acquired by the Lighthouse Bureau and became the station's official residence. (The bungalow, abandoned with the light's automation, burned in the early 1990s.)

The station went into operation in December 1889. Its fog bell had once been used at one of the West's earliest lighthouses. The 1,600-pound bell, cast in Philadelphia in 1855, was first used at Cape Disappointment in 1856. From there it was sent to Puget Sound's West Point Lighthouse in 1881. The bell was struck by a mechanism that worked like a big grandfather clock, its 1,500-pound weight suspended from a cable that was wound by hand.

The first keeper at the Warrior Rock Lighthouse, Joseph Hayburn, noted "trouble with the bell" in his early log book entries, as well as the fact that the "lamp kept blowing out." Later log book entries described the river as "full of running ice" and told of occasional ice blockages when ships could not run the river.

Keepers also wrote of the daily rate of the river's rise and fall. At times of flooding, the water frequently rose some twenty-five feet to the bottom of the wooden tower, completely covering the rock. The keepers then used the station's boat to reach the tower to tend the lamp and fog signal. They used the same boat to go to Saint Helens for supplies and mail.

Frank DeRoy became the keeper in 1925. The DeRoys transferred from Heceta Head to Warrior Rock so that their ten-year-old son Bob could receive orthodontic work in Portland. In a letter to the U.S. Lighthouse Society, Bob DeRoy recalled his days at the station:

"By taking the steamer *America* on its regular run in the morning, picking up milk along the way from dairy ranches along the river, I could get the necessary [orthodontic] work done, and return in the afternoon [to Saint Helens] from Portland."

When the DeRoys first arrived at the station, the tower still had the oil lamp and the hand-cranked striking mechanism for the bell. DeRoy recalls his father thinking that there had to be a better way than rowing out to the tower at times of high water. Keeper DeRoy rigged a cable from the tower to a tree close to the living quarters, about 200 feet from the tower. Then he suspended a basket from the cable. By sitting in the basket, he could pull himself to and from the tower.

Frank DeRoy retired from the Lighthouse Service in 1935 at age sixty-five. During his tenure, the wooden tower was replaced by a cement tower with the old bell and a light on top. Electricity also came to the station before DeRoy retired. He no longer had to walk along the rock or ride in his basket to reach the tower. Instead, he could activate both bell and light with a switch in his home.

On a May morning in 1969, a barge was being towed past the rock when the towline snapped. Swinging against the tower, the barge broke open the tower's masonry shell and exposed the rubble base. To repair the tower, the Coast Guard began by removing the bell and its striking mechanism. As they did this, the bell was damaged, and parts of it and the striking mechanism were lost in the river.

For a time, the damaged bell sat in a Columbia County road shop while Roy A. Perry, of the county's historical society, researched its history. Local divers probed the waters around the rock and found some of the missing pieces. The historic bell was repaired and placed on permanent display in the small square in front of the county courthouse, which is also the home of the society's museum.

Behind the courthouse there is a one-half scale replica of the original tower. One can imagine keeper DeRoy pulling himself towards it, above the swirling waters, then scrambling inside to activate the bell.

Directions and Hours: The courthouse is east of Highway 30. Follow the "Historic District" signs. The Columbia County Historical Society museum hours are noon to 4:00 P.M., Fridays and Saturdays. The small lighthouse tower is obscured from the riverfront by Warrior Point.

OREGON HISTORICAL SOCIETY-76682

**The Willamette River Lighthouse stood near the river's confluence
with the Columbia.**

Chapter 14

Willamette River Lighthouse

Where the Willamette River flows into the mighty Columbia, a lighthouse and fog signal were built in 1895. Forty years later the station was abandoned, and today it no longer exists. Its short career marked a phase in assisting river navigators that began with only a few unlighted buoys.

In 1866 the Lighthouse Board was receiving complaints about its lack of attention to the buoys in the Columbia River. The Board said it was seeking to remedy "the evils pointed out," but noted that the transfer of the West Coast's only tender, the *Shubrick*, to other duties during the Civil War prevented the placement of new buoys.

The *Shubrick* returned to lighthouse duty in 1866, but in 1867 the Board noted that the shifting of the river's channels made proper placement of the buoys difficult. In 1868 there were only eleven unlighted buoys marking the two channels at the Columbia's mouth. A few more marked a channel twenty-five miles upriver.

In the 1870s the U.S. Army Corps of Engineers began to improve the Columbia and Willamette rivers by dredging channels and damming sloughs. During this decade, the Lighthouse Service placed more buoys and began establishing unlighted marks to assist mariners in entering and following channels.

Beginning with the first nighttime aids at the Saint Helens bar in 1877, the Lighthouse Service added more small lanterns along the rivers. By 1892 there were thirty-eight river lights from the Columbia's mouth to Portland, a distance of nearly 115 miles. The Board said these lights "have revolutionized steamboat navigation, making it almost as easy and as safe to run by night as by day."

Two such lights had been placed on small islands near the Willamette's mouth in 1883, but in 1892 the Lighthouse Board described the channel's entrance as narrow, and said that vessels entering the Willamette "have at times in foggy weather great difficulty . . . causing much delay and inconvenience." A lighthouse and fog signal were proposed for the site, and Congress authorized construction funds in 1894.

The site for the station was purchased from the Pearcy family for one dollar. Located at the Willamette's mouth, near today's Kelly Point, the plot was on a small island that was often submerged by spring floods. The lighthouse, completed in December of 1895, was built on a rectangular cluster of piles driven into the sand. The two-story, octagonal building had a widow's walk on top with the light mounted in its center. Dormers protruded from the second story roof. Below, a fog bell with a striking mechanism was mounted on the porch.

Water for the station was delivered by steamer and pumped up to a holding tank. The station had a rowboat, and at low water the keeper climbed down a twenty-four-foot ladder to reach the craft before rowing to town for mail and groceries.

According to marine writer Larry Barber, the station saw a succession of keepers during its forty years of service. The most colorful was German immigrant Herman Halkett, who proudly strode the widow's walk in his Lighthouse Service uniform. Keeper Jerome Webster extinguished the light in 1935.

In that year, according to Barber, the light and fog signal were moved to the end of a 500-foot-long pile dike built northerly into the river from Kelly Point. The light and fog signal were electrified and no longer needed a keeper's care. The Lighthouse Bureau declared the original building and land to be surplus property. In 1939 the Lighthouse Bureau tried to sell the building to someone who would move it away, but there were no takers.

The old lighthouse was given a second life when it was acquired by the Portland Merchants Exchange in the 1940s. A barge crane lifted and swung the dwelling to a new location on low piling on a Kelly Point beach — a move that was featured in a 1946 pictorial story in New York's *Sunday News*.

The new residents of the dwelling would need the same diligence as the lighthouse keepers had demonstrated. On behalf of the Exchange, they notified their Portland office of arriving ships so linesmen and stevedores could be ready at the docks in Portland when the ships came in.

Al Swanson and his wife were serving there during the disastrous Vanport Flood of 1949. Reluctant to leave their post, they spent two nights tethered to the building in rubber rafts as the water rose into the building.

In the 1950s, the Merchants Exchange built a new station on Sauvie Island. Once again the lighthouse was abandoned — this time for the last time. Soon after, the building was destroyed by fire.

Today the Willamette flows broadly into the Columbia. Only Warrior Rock's tower stands as a reminder of the river's three manned lighthouses. Where once there were only a handful of unlighted buoys and lanterns, there are now over 300 automated lights to mark the mariner's way from the Columbia's entrance to Portland.

History meets at the Columbia River Maritime Museum. The last Columbia River Lightship is moored near a large navigational buoy like the one that replaced it. Behind are the masts of the replica of the *Lady Washington* in port for a brief visit.

Section 5

Ships and Signals

Oregon's surviving lighthouses are tangible evidence of the state's maritime history. More evidence can be seen in the lightship moored at Astoria's Columbia River Maritime Museum. It is the last in a long line of Columbia River Lightships that marked the river's entrance. Less evident are the roles played by lighthouse tenders, and the history of the gleaming Fresnel lenses and the resounding fog signals.

Lighthouse tenders, sailing from a lighthouse depot, steamed thousands of miles each year to bring supplies to the remote lighthouse stations and lightships. Together, the tenders and the depot formed a lighthouse lifeline.

The Fresnel lens, first displayed in France in 1822, would seem obsolete today, but even when used with a whale oil lamp it could cast beams of light as far to sea as modern beacons.

Except for fog bells displayed in museums, there is little evidence left of the signals of sound that once guided mariners through Oregon's fogs. The steam boilers and their whistles, sirens, and Daboll trumpets are long removed, replaced by electric horns.

The stories about these ships and signals will enrich any visitor's exploration of lighthouses along the Oregon Coast.

COLUMBIA RIVER MARITIME MUSEUM

The first Columbia River lightship is readied for its overland trip to the Columbia River after grounding on an ocean beach.

Chapter 15

Columbia River Lightships

A lightship dropped its 5,000-pound, mushroom-shaped anchor off the Columbia River's entrance for the first time on April 11, 1892. Most of its 900 feet of iron anchor chain was paid out against the Pacific's swells. This was the West Coast's first lightship. Eventually, four more lightship stations were established: two in California and two in Washington.

Lightships were floating lighthouses. They marked dangerous reefs and banks, or the entrances to rivers or bays. Like their shorebound sisters, they displayed lights and fog signals with characteristics particular to each station. Their keepers were the ships' crews.

Early U.S. lightships were numbered in the order in which they were built, and the Columbia River's first lightship was officially known as Light Vessel *No. 50*. The 112-foot-long vessel's two coal-fired boilers produced steam for a twelve-inch whistle and condensed fresh water from the sea. Three lenses with oil lamps encircled each of the ship's two masts. To help mariners recognize the ship as a navigational aid in daytime, distinctive circular panels were mounted atop the masts, and the wood-planked hull was painted bright red.

Built in San Francisco, the lightship had no engines, but carried sails for emergencies. It was towed to its position, about eight miles southwest of Cape Disappointment, by the lighthouse tender *Manzanita*. The lightship was soon moved about three miles to the southwest. This helped vessels approaching the Columbia from the south. Also, the Lighthouse Board said that from this location, if the vessel broke loose, it likely could be sailed safely into the river.

In fact, the move had little effect on the lightship's safety. On November 28, 1899, a severe storm struck the Oregon Coast. Towards evening, the lightship's anchor chain broke. As waves hammered the ship, the crew set its sails and managed to keep the vessel at sea until morning, when help arrived.

The tug *Wallula* got a heavy line to the lightship, but it quickly broke. The *Manzanita* then secured a line that also broke, getting wrapped in the tender's propeller. The tug *Escort* got a third line to the embattled lightship and had almost pulled it to safety inside the bar when that line snapped.

The lightship was blown toward McKenzie Head, a rocky promontory west of Cape Disappointment. A crescent of sand lay between the head and the cape, and the lightship's officers decided to try to beach the ship there in order to save it and the crew. On the evening of November 29, the ship drove against the sand. With skillful handling of the sails, the crew managed to get the ship's prow turned seaward to breast the incoming waves. Everyone on board was rescued, but the lightship lay stranded on the beach.

The ship, suffering little damage, held fast to the sand. Attempts to pull it off the beach were unsuccessful. The vessel swung broadside to the waves and begin to fill with sand.

Intent on salvaging the lightship, the Lighthouse Board decided that it could somehow be moved overland to the Columbia River. The Portland house-moving firm of Roberts and Allen thought this was possible and successfully bid the contract.

In April 1901 the house-movers jacked a cradle under the vessel, and turned its prow toward a path cleared to the Columbia River, 700 yards away. With block and tackle and capstans turned by horses, the 300-ton ship was slowly winched across the isthmus to safety. On June 2 it was triumphantly launched into the river's Baker Bay.

After being repaired in Portland, the lightship returned to its station on August 18, 1901. The name "Columbia," painted in bold, white letters, was displayed on both sides of the hull.

In 1909 a new lightship marked "Columbia" steamed into position to replace *No. 50*. This new ship, *No. 88*, had a steel hull and a propeller driven by a steam engine. Built on the East Coast, it made the trip to San Francisco in 124 days under its own power. Its lights were oil lanterns hoisted on each masthead; its fog signal was a twelve-inch steam chime.

The first master of the new Columbia River Lightship was Captain

Jacob Nielsen. In a 1951 newspaper article he recounted his many years on the vessel. Nielsen received a commendation from the Lighthouse Service in 1913 for assistance provided after the tanker *Rosecrans* sank near the Columbia's entrance. Thirty-three persons lost their lives, but two survivors and the crew of a lifesaving boat were brought to safety on the lightship in heaving seas.

Nielsen also told of an elderly Chinese cook who once served under him. The cook prided himself on his immaculate galley and the punctuality of his meals. One evening, just before dinner, a wave crashed through the galley's skylight. Pots and pans washed about amid shattered glass. Nielsen recalled the crew laughing as the cook stammered in frustration, his routine broken.

Fixing a broken skylight could be handled by the ship's carpenter, but when storms caused serious damage, the lightship came to shore for repairs. While the regular lightships were off-station, relief vessels took their place. With "Relief" painted on their sides, these lightships, like chameleons, could change their light and fog signal characteristics to match those of the vessels they replaced.

During its four decades stationed at the entrance of the Columbia River, Light Vessel *No. 88* underwent many changes. The ship was equipped with a radio in 1920 and a radio beacon in 1924. In 1927 electric lights replaced the kerosene lamps, and in the 1930s a diesel electric engine replaced the old steam engine. Replaced by another lightship in 1939, *No. 88* was assigned to Washington's Umatilla Reef station, where it finished its career in 1960.

In 1951 a new Columbia River Lightship, *WAL 604*, arrived. It was one of the last lightships to be built in the United States. At 112 feet in length, it was powered by a 550-horsepower diesel engine. Electric lights — in later years, a cluster of twenty-four locomotive headlights — shone from the mainmast.

Though on a modern vessel, crews found life aboard the new lightship to be much like that experienced by their predecessors. Like earlier ships, the modern vessel vibrated with each blast of the fog horn, and sleep was difficult as the vessel rolled. In winds above fifty knots, the engine growled constantly as the ship powered into the anchor to hold its position.

Unlike the men in Captain Nielsen's time, who would stay aboard for up to ninety days, these crews were on station for only two to three weeks before going ashore, and they had television and radio to entertain them. Yet boredom was still a problem. To fill the hours, the crew played cards and chess, and pursued hobbies. Fishing was popular, and most of the cooks became adept at canning fish to be given to family or friends ashore.

Sometimes the boredom was broken by sheer terror. The greatest danger was a collision with a passing ship. The crew of the lightship was drilled to get under way in one and one-half minutes if the radar picked up a ship on a collision course. One night the alarm sounded, and crewman Robert Grey ran forward to his station to slacken the anchor chain. A ship under tow passed by in the gloom; "I could have reached out and written my name on it," Grey said later.

The lightship era began to end in the 1960s. One by one the vessels were retired, replaced by large, automated buoys. In December 1979, *WAL 604* pulled its anchor from the Columbia River Station, the last of the five West Coast stations to be automated.

Since the era's beginning in 1892, nine different vessels, including relief ships, had served on the three Northwest lightship stations. When the era ended, few of the ships remained. Most had been sold and scraped at the close of their careers.

Flags and pennants flew as groups and individuals tried to save the few lightships that were left. Captain Nielsen's vessel, *No. 88*, was rescued from the scrapyard by the Columbia River Maritime Museum in 1963. In 1979 it was sold to a Cathlament, Washington, restauranteur. His business failed, and the ship was sold and taken to eastern Canada.

The sale of *No. 88* made room at the museum's dock for *WAL 604*. This last Columbia River lightship is a popular attraction at the museum. It is kept in a condition that would have pleased Captain Nielsen's Chinese cook — immaculate through and through.

Directions and Hours: *WAL 604* is moored at the Columbia River Maritime Museum in Astoria, Oregon. This waterfront museum is east of the Columbia River Bridge at 1792 Marine Drive. It is open daily from 9:30 A.M. to 5 P.M. except on Thanksgiving and Christmas. Phone: (503) 325-2323.

Chapter 16

Lighthouse Lifelines

The early keepers of Oregon's lights were residents of government outposts often akin in remoteness to frontier military posts. Instead of watching for the dusty approach of quartermaster supply trains, the keepers and their families watched for the smoke and flags that signaled the arrival of the lighthouse tender.

These steadfast vessels brought fuel for the lamps and boilers, as well as provisions, catalogs, and news of fellow keepers. The inspector was on board, too. Along with the keepers' pay, he brought a keen eye, ready to ensure that the station was being operated according to a host of strict regulations.

To the lightships, the tenders brought supplies and fresh crews to relieve the weary men, tired by a long stint at sea. In addition, tenders carried construction supplies to new lighthouse stations, and set and tended channel-marking buoys and minor beacons.

Over the years, many lighthouse tenders served on Oregon's waters. Like the lighthouses and lightships, each developed a character and a distinctive history of its own.

The first was the sidewheel steamer *Shubrick*. Built in Philadelphia in 1857, the 140-foot-long vessel, rigged as a brigantine when under sail, made a five-month voyage through the Straits of Magellan and churned into San Francisco Bay in May 1858. There were then sixteen lighthouse stations to tend along the West Coast, but one of the ship's first tasks was to place buoys from the entrance of the Columbia River to Astoria.

During the Civil War the *Shubrick* was assigned to the U.S. Revenue

Service in customs and law enforcement duties, and in 1865 it joined a U.S. Navy expedition to the Bering Straits. A year later the ship was returned to the Lighthouse Service.

Many new lighthouses were built in the period following the Civil War, and by 1879 thirty-seven lighthouses stood on the West Coast from San Diego to Puget Sound. The *Shubrick* was still the only tender, trying to reach each station at least every three months, while caring for buoys and minor beacons as well.

Relief came in 1880 when a new tender arrived to tend the lighthouses in California. A steam screw tender (its propeller was powered by a steam engine), the *Manzanita* was the first in a long line of tenders named for plants. The *Shubrick*'s responsibilities were narrowed to the stations in Oregon, Washington, and Alaska.

By then the Lighthouse Service had established a small lighthouse depot on the Columbia River. The depot served as a place to repair buoys and to store supplies and coal for delivery to the lighthouses and lightships. The five-acre property, with over 500 feet of waterfront, was near Astoria at Tongue Point. The site had been purchased in 1876 for $100 in gold coin.

Meanwhile, the twenty-three-year-old *Shubrick* was showing its age. By 1885 its worn-out boilers could no longer lift a first-class buoy. The following year, the *Manzanita* came north, replaced in California by the tender *Madrono*. The *Shubrick* was sold and eventually burned on a mud flat in San Francisco Bay.

In 1893 the *Columbine* was assigned to assist the *Manzanita*, especially to make the long summer trips to tend Alaska's buoys and channel beacons. By then the depot at Tongue Point was being upgraded. For several years the Lighthouse Board had considered moving the depot to Astoria. But in 1891 the Board found that Astoria "has great immediate expectations. The prices asked for its waterfront property have advanced greatly." Unable to find an affordable site, the funds authorized for the move were used for improvements at Tongue Point.

A new tender, the *Heather*, arrived at the depot in 1903 to join the *Manzanita* and the *Columbine*. During the following year, the three tenders built an imposing record in the service of stations in Washington, Oregon, and Alaska. They traveled a combined total of 44,000 miles, delivered 894 tons of coal and 884 tons of supplies, and tended 324 buoys and beacons.

The hard-working trio was broken up in 1905 when the *Manzanita*, rammed by a dredge under tow, sank in the Columbia River. It took nearly three years to build a replacement vessel, also named the *Manzanita*.

The new steel-hulled ship, 190 feet long, retained the classic lines and characteristics of earlier steam screw tenders. A tall smokestack stood amidships. Though auxiliary sails were no longer necessary, it carried two masts. The foremast, with a boom attached, acted as a derrick crane. A spacious foredeck had room for buoys, and a large hold below could store supplies. Staterooms swept aft behind a wheel house, providing cabins for the inspector, the captain, and the keepers and their families on their way to new assignments.

Although their main duty was to service lighthouse stations, sometimes tenders came to the rescue of entire communities. In December 1922, the second *Manzanita* lay at an Astoria dock, ready for an early morning departure down the Oregon Coast. At 2:30 A.M. the ship's watch reported a fire in the town's business district. The ship's commander, Captain A. A. Modeer, steamed up the tender and headed toward the flames.

Using the ship's pumps and hoses, the crew first saved a warehouse, then an apartment building. Then the crew helped save the old Parker Hotel, preventing the fire from reaching oil tanks only a few blocks away.

Eight years later, the *Manzanita* came to the rescue a second time. The tender was at Astoria in January 1930 when a rare period of sub-freezing temperatures locked the Columbia River in ice. Four to ten inches thick, the ice froze ships in place from Portland to thirty miles downriver.

On January 17 the *Manzanita* broke its way to Portland and spent four days freeing icebound ships in the harbor. Returning downriver, the tender freed more ships on the way. By the time the vessel reached Tongue Point, urgent requests for aid were being received from isolated island communities on the lower river.

This time the tender *Rose*, built in 1916, went upriver with the Coast Guard cutter *Northwind*. The shallow draft *Rose* maneuvered its boom, hung with a dead weight, to rock its way through the jammed ice. The ships delivered supplies and food for livestock to nine icebound communities.

Like the *Manzanita*, the *Rose* also encountered fire. Flames gutted the town of Bandon in September 1936. In port to service the Coquille River Lighthouse, the ship's launch and the cargo boat were used to ferry refugees

The lighthouse tender *Rose* assisted survivors of the disastrous Bandon fire in 1936.

to safety on the river's north side. Over 200 people crowded aboard the tender at the height of the fire.

In spite of such heroics, the day of the lighthouse tenders was coming to a close. As electricity reached the lighthouses and roads were improved, the need for lighthouse tenders diminished. The ships grew old, and the fleet gradually disappeared as the tenders were retired.

Today U.S. Coast Guard buoy tenders carry on the tradition set by the *Shubrick*, the *Manzanita*, and the *Rose*. Still named for plants, these vessels no longer visit the automated lighthouses. Like their predecessors, they do some rescue work, but their main role is to maintain the buoys that are critical to safe navigation.

The buoy tender *Iris* is stationed at Tongue Point. This 180-foot-ship, built in 1943, has a compliment of fifty-four officers and men. The *Iris* tends aids to navigation along Oregon's coast and partway up the lower Columbia. The smaller *Bluebell*, stationed at Portland, tends the marks farther upriver.

On a windy afternoon one might catch a glimpse of the *Iris* headed to Tongue Point, its foredeck piled with buoys needing repair. It serves as a reminder of the days when the *Shubrick* churned up the river to the depot as a part of the lighthouse lifeline.

TED NELSON

A young visitor peers into Cape Disappointment's original first-order Fresnel lens, displayed at the Lewis and Clark Interpretive Center.

Chapter 17

Beams of Light

The beams of light that guided early mariners along Oregon's coast came from a lens designed in the early 1800s. Yet this system of lenses and prisms, combined with an oil-burning lamp, produced a powerful beam.

Designed by Augustin Fresnel (pronounced *Fray-nell*) and known as the Fresnel lens, the system was first used in France in 1822. Four of these lenses, now used with electric lamps, still guide mariners along Oregon's waters.

Fresnel was born in France in 1788. Wayne Wheeler, in the U. S. Lighthouse Society's *The Keepers Log*, described him as a frail man plagued by ill health. He died at the age of thirty-nine. After doing poorly in early school, he developed an aptitude for mathematics and geometry. He pursued an interest in light and optics while employed as a road engineer. Using drops of honey for lenses and the sun for light, he gradually developed the theories that led to the design of his lens.

After its first use in France, the lens was quickly adopted by most seacoast nations of the world — except the United States. At this time, the Fifth Auditor of the Treasury was in charge of U.S. lighthouses. Unwilling to spend the money for new lenses, he stubbornly stuck to a cheaper, inferior system, developed in 1810, that used Argand lamps and parabolic reflectors.

Failure to use the Fresnel lens was one symptom of the inadequacies in the country's lighthouse system. Congress began to look into the problems in 1837, but except for the testing of two Fresnel lenses, no significant improvements were made.

In 1851, with more and more mariners complaining, Congress convened a board to investigate the Fifth Auditor's department. The investigation led to the establishment of a Lighthouse Board in 1852. One of the Board's first actions was to adopt the Fresnel lens for use in all U.S. lighthouses.

Fresnel's lens consisted of a central lens, a light source located at the center of the lens' focal plane, and a system of dioptric and catadioptric prisms. The dioptric prisms captured light not focused by the central lens and refracted it outward into a parallel, horizontal beam. The catadioptric prisms captured the more oblique rays of light and refracted and reflected them outward. The result was a powerful sheet of horizontal light. A beam from the largest lens could be seen more than twenty miles at sea.

Lenses were made in different sizes called "orders." The largest, used in seacoast towers, were of the first order. Six feet in diameter and ten to twelve feet high, they weighed over four tons. Smaller, fourth-order lenses were about three feet high and about twenty inches in diameter. They were used mainly for harbor entrance lights.

Regardless of its size, each lens was made in brass framed sections. The frames were inscribed with numbers so the lenses, built in France or England, could be shipped in sections and easily reassembled in the lighthouse tower.

The design of the lens allowed each light to display a characteristic which distinguished it from other lights. Fixed lights were produced by a lens with a convex belt of glass wrapped around the circumference, with the prisms arrayed above and below. Sometimes called a "drum lens," it cast a constant beam.

Flashing lights were produced by a rotating lens with from two to twenty-four panels. In each panel, a circular, convex lens, called a "bullseye," was surrounded by the prisms. As the lens turned, each panel cast a concentrated beam of light with dark intervals between. The lens with its panels were mounted on wheels or on ball bearings, or floated in a bed of mercury. It was turned by a hand-wound clockwork mechanism, or, later, by electric motors. The light's characteristic could be varied by using different combinations of lighted and blank panels and/or colored screens.

Sometimes a rotating lens would combine the features of a fixed lens and a flashing lens. It would produce a constant beam of light occasionally interrupted by a brilliant flash.

Other variations of Fresnel's design, on a small scale, were used for minor lights that marked hazards or channels. Called "lens lanterns" and "post lights," they were usually tended by contracted lamp lighters. These workers filled the lamp's reservoirs with several days supply of fuel, delivered by lighthouse tender.

The light source for the early lenses were lamps, some with up to five wicks, which required careful trimming. A chimney enclosing the wicks needed constant cleaning.

The lamps were fueled with whale oil at first. In the mid-1850s this oil became so expensive that substitutes were sought. Beginning in the 1860s, lard oil became the preferred fuel; it was replaced by kerosene in the late 1870s. In 1898 the incandescent oil vapor lamp was introduced. Operating like a Coleman lantern, it was the last major innovation before electricity came to the lighthouses.

Like the lenses they held, the lighthouse towers were great feats of design and engineering. They did much more than merely raise the lens to increase the light's range. Their other functions can best be appreciated by taking a tour of a typical seacoast tower with a rotating lens.

At the base of the tower, the visitor enters the workroom. Here the keeper stored tools, supplies, cloths, and polishing materials for the lens and its brass. Off the workroom, a spiral staircase winds up into the gloom of the double-walled tower, designed to withstand hurricane-force winds. Before sunset each day, the keeper carried about five gallons of fuel from the separate oil house into the tower and up the steep steps.

At the next-to-last landing, the visitor enters the watchroom. The pedestal, supporting the lens above, stands in the room's center. An electric motor now turns the lens, replacing the clockwork mechanism that the keepers once wound by hand to rotate the lens. Here the keeper stood his watch and, every day, cleaned the night's accumulation of soot off the lamp's chimney. In the keeper's time, a smock would have hung on the wall, the required dress for cleaning the lens.

Up the last flight of stairs, the visitor enters the lantern room to gaze at the lens and at the ocean below. This room is surrounded by storm panes of thick glass that protect the lens from the elements. The panes, held in place by metal frames, comprise the tower's lantern. Outside, above the gallery, the frames have handholds to assist the keeper while he cleaned salt spray from the lantern.

The lens, turning quietly on its wheels, is lit by a small electric bulb in place of the original oil lamp. In the keeper's time, the lens was used only at night. During the day it was shrouded by a curtain to protect the lens from the sun's rays.

Parts of the early system are no longer used or have been removed from the modernized tower. Near the base of the lantern room are vents that, when carefully adjusted, provided a draft to clear condensation from the lantern and improve the efficiency of the lamp. A vent tube, now removed, carried the lamp's fumes out to a ball vent on top of the tower's metalclad dome. When properly adjusted, the entire system acted like a giant chimney.

Leaving the lantern room and descending the spiral staircase, the visitor finds it easier to envision the thousands of times the same steps were taken by lighthouse keepers as they tended Fresnel's lens.

Chapter 18

Signals of Sound

Oregon's lighthouse visitors may sometimes be unable to see the top of the tower in the thick summertime fog that often envelops the coast. On such days, the visitor gains a sense of the importance that fog signals had for mariners groping along the coast in near-zero visibility.

Nine of Oregon's lighthouse stations had fog signals at some time in their careers. The first fog signals were bells. A bell placed at Cape Disappointment could not be heard from the high point, and the first Umpqua River station had a bell that also proved ineffective because it couldn't be heard over the noise of the surf. Bells were later used effectively at two Columbia River stations where audible range was less important as ships passed close by.

Experiments with more effective sound devices were begun in the 1850s, and by the mid-1860s new equipment was being developed. The experiments confirmed that sound carries unevenly through the atmosphere, so sounds that could be heard at great distances were sometimes faint or silent closer to the signal. These anomalies often varied with the weather. The experiments led to the use of three sound signals — the siren, the Daboll trumpet, and the steam whistle — but each had its own limitations.

An example is the siren used at Tillamook Rock. It consisted of two trumpets (one used for back-up), each about seventeen feet long with a small throat and a flaring mouth nearly three feet across. The sound was created by steam being forced through a slotted, fixed plate and a rotating disk.

Major George Gillespie, who built the signal, tested it soon after construction. He found the sound became practically inaudible two to seven miles from the station, but then could be heard again from seven to eleven miles away.

Daboll trumpets were used at Coquille River, Cape Arago, and Desdemona Sands. They also had large trumpets, but the sound was produced in a resonating cavity by a steel reed being vibrated by hot air or steam. This created a shriek that was most effective along the trumpet's axis.

The steam whistle at Point Adams was similar to the metal cylindrical signals used on locomotives. It radiated a strong sound in all directions, but was hard on boilers and was slow to go into action if fog appeared quickly.

Experiments in the 1880s rated the fog signals by their sound-producing power. The siren rated highest, then the steam whistle, then the Daboll trumpet. The devices could be rated in the same order according to the amount of fuel they consumed.

Lighthouse keepers knew this difference well. Over a three-year period in the 1890s, Tillamook Rock's siren sounded for 524 hours. Every fifteen hours of operation, the keepers stoked the boiler with a ton of coal. In contrast, Coquille's Daboll trumpet shrieked for 1,204 hours during this same period, but it could run for fifty hours on a ton of coal.

In the early 1900s, oil replaced coal as fuel, and new technologies allowed sound to be cast across the water more effectively. Today's electric fog signals are automated, activated by equipment that detects moisture in the air.

Gone are the dusty, noisy boilers of the early fog signals that stood in stark contrast to the polished brass and sparkling prisms of the lens. However, the sounds the signals produced were as welcome to mariners in the fog as the lens' beams were on a fogless night.

Lighthouse Summary

Cape Arago: Chapter 3. Established 1866. Reestablished 1909 and again in 1934. Modern optic in third tower. Grounds closed. View from south of Sunset Bay State Park.

Cape Blanco: Chapter 1. Established 1870. Original tower with operating Fresnel lens. Grounds closed. View from west boundary of Cape Blanco State Park.

Cape Disappointment: Chapter 11. Established 1856. Original tower with operating fourth-order Fresnel lens. Grounds open. Original first-order Fresnel lens displayed at Lewis and Clark Interpertive Center, Fort Canby State Park, Washington.

Cape Meares: Chapter 8. Established 1890. Original tower with original first-order lens. Operating light is a modern optic. Grounds open year-round and tower open in summer months. Cape Meares State Park.

Coquille River: Chapter 2. Established 1896. Discontinued 1939. Original lens removed. Fog signal room and grounds open. Bullards Beach State Park.

Desdemona Sands: Chapter 12. Established 1902. Discontinued 1934 as a keepers' station. Nothing remains.

Heceta Head: Chapter 5. Established 1894. Original keepers' dwelling and tower with operating, original first-order Fresnel lens. Grounds open. Near Devils Elbow State Park.

Point Adams: Chapter 10. Established 1875. Discontinued 1899. Nothing remains.

Tillamook Rock: Chapter 9. Established 1881. Discontinued 1957. Private columbarium. View from Ecola State Park, Cannon Beach, and Seaside.

Warrior Rock: Chapter 13. Established 1889. Small tower with modern optic. View by boat one mile southeast of Saint Helens. Original fog bell at Saint Helens Courthouse.

Willamette River: Chapter 14. Established 1895. Discontinued 1935. Nothing remains.

Umpqua River: Chapter 4. Established 1857. Destroyed by floods 1863. Reestablished 1894. Second tower with operating first-order Fresnel lens. View from park roadway. Umpqua River Lighthouse State Park.

Yaquina Bay: Chapter 6. Established 1871. Discontinued 1873. Original lens removed. Lighthouse restored. Open as a museum. Yaquina Bay State Park.

Yaquina Head: Chapter 7. Established 1873. Original tower with operating, original first-order Fresnel lens. Grounds open. Summer tower tours. Yaquina Head Outstanding Natural Area.

Index

115

Further Reading

Beckham, Stephen Dow. *Land of the Umpqua: A History of Douglas County, Oregon.* Roseburg, Oregon: Douglas County Commissioners, 1986.

Finucane, Stephanie. *Heceta House: A History and Architectural Survey.* Waldport, Oregon: Siuslaw National Forest, 1980.

Gibbs, James A. *Tillamook Light.* Portland, Oregon: Binford & Mort Publishing, 1979.

Oregon's Seacoast Lighthouses. Medford, Oregon: Webb Research Group, 1992.

Hays, Marjorie H. *The Land That Kept Its Promise.* Newport, Oregon: Lincoln County Historical Society, 1976.

Holland, Francis Ross, Jr. *America's Lighthouses: An Illustrated History.* New York: Dover Publications, Inc., 1972.

Marshall, Don. *Oregon Shipwrecks.* Portland, Oregon: Binford & Mort Publishing, 1984.

Nelson, Sharlene P. and Ted W. *Cruising the Columbia and Snake Rivers.* Seattle, Washington: Pacific Search Press, 1981, revised 1986.

Umbrella Guide to Washington Lighthouses. Seattle, Washington: Epicenter Press, 1990.

Umbrella Guide to California Lighthouses. Seattle, Washington: Epicenter Press, 1993.

Roberts, Bruce and Jones, Ray. *Western Lighthouses.* Old Saybrook, Connecticut: The Globe Pequot Press, 1993.

About the Authors

S harlene and Ted Nelson found the genesis for this book at their kitchen table. One morning, over coffee, the couple was considering new topics to write about. From their Puget Sound home, Ted gazed across the water to the lighthouse at Point Robinson and said, "How about a book on lighthouses?" That thought led to Umbrella Guides about the lighthouses of Washington and California and now this book about Oregon lighthouses.

Writing about lighthouses was a spontaneous idea, but not an idle one. The Nelsons had been studying and writing about regional and maritime history for nearly forty years. After graduating from the University of California, Berkeley, the couple delved into logging history while Ted worked as a resident forester in a northern California logging camp. Moving to Washington, they continued to write about early logging history and other topics as well.

While living in eastern North Carolina, they chronicled the history of that area. Later, Sharlene served as a correspondent for *The Oregonian* while the couple lived in Coos Bay, Oregon, and Longview, Washington. Their first book, *Cruising the Columbia and Snake Rivers*, was published in 1981.

Ted and Sharlene sail, backpack, and ski, often with their two grandchildren.